BRYANT'S MAP OF NORFOLK

IN 1826

With an introduction and analysis by

J.C.Barringer

Larks Press

Published by
The Larks Press
Ordnance Farmhouse, Guist Bottom, Dereham,
Norfolk NR20 5PF
Tel./Fax. 01328 829207

E-mail: larkspress@talk21.com

Printed by the Lanceni Press, Fakenham

First printed July 1998
Reprinted 1999, 2000, 2002 & 2004

ACKNOWLEDGEMENTS

The publishers wish to thank Dr Peter Wade-Martins who kindly lent his copy of the map so that negatives could be made; David Urry of Big Camera, Norwich, who photographed the map; George Broughton of Lanceni Press who assisted with the design; David Yaxley who drew the Key; Chris Barringer who not only wrote the introduction, but constantly reminded us that the project was waiting to be done!

Faden's Map of Norfolk, 1797, also published by the Larks Press, is still available at £6.95.

British Library Cataloguing-in-publication Data.
A catalogue record for this book is available from the British Library

ISBN 0 948400 71 4

Introduction

On December 1st 1826 Andrew Bryant published his new map of the County of Norfolk from an 'Actual Survey' carried out in 1824, 1825 and 1826. This was one of twelve county maps he published between 1822, when he produced his map of Hert-fordshire, and 1835, when he published his map of Herefordshire. (See p.82)

The period from 1770 until 1840 was one of great map-making activity in Great Britain and Ireland. In Norfolk, Hochstetter produced his splendid plan of Norwich in 1789 and Faden published the first one inch to one mile (1: 63,360) map of the county in 1797;[1] then in 1836-7 the Ordnance Survey brought out their first one-inch sheets of the county. The Board of Ordnance, later to be known as the Ordnance Survey (hereafter O.S.) had carried out surveying in Norfolk in 1816 and 1817.[2] Bryant's map, unlike Faden's, therefore overlapped with the mapping being carried out by the O.S.

The production of twelve county maps, several of which were being mapped at the same time, points to Bryant having highly-organised teams of surveyors at work. On all his maps he refers to 'An Actual Survey' and Harley has suggested that the triangulation work being carried out by the O.S. may have been available. The remarkable speed with which Greenwood, Bryant and Teesdale were producing county maps is striking, and Harley comments that 'such speed was partly facilitated by the basic ready-made triangulations (by the O.S.), but also accomplished, less creditably, through the neglect of thorough topographical mapping.'[3]

The period from 1770, when large-scale maps of one inch to a mile or more began to appear, was one in which wealthy patrons were needed who were prepared to subscribe to the pro-duction of a map so that field survey work could be carried out. Bryant does not acknowledge a particular patron for his Norfolk map, simply the 'Nobility, Clergy and Gentry' of the county, whereas his Suffolk map, also published in 1826, was dedicated to 'His Grace the Duke of Grafton, Lord Lieutenant'. Norfolk's gentry may well have become chary of sponsoring a new map after M.J.Armstrong failed to complete his map c.1786 after many had subscribed to it.[4] Faden did, however, pick up the project and completed it by 1797.

All Bryant's maps were published from 27, Great Ormond Street in London and Harley notes that he finally went out of business in 1835 after producing his Herefordshire map. This was the result of the increased effectiveness of the Ordnance Survey and the support it received from government: private map-makers could not compete at the one-inch scale. In fact Bryant's map is at rather more than the one-inch scale; it is described as being at a scale of 10 miles to 12 ¼ inches. This is a scale of 1:51,742 which makes Bryant an interesting map to compare with the present O.S. Landranger sheets with the modern 1:50,000 scale. It also means that it appears less 'cluttered' than Faden's map. Bryant did not adhere to one scale; his Bedford map of 1826 had a scale of 1:42,500 and his Buckinghamshire map one of 1: 40,000.[5]

The O.S. carried out their field mapping at a scale of 2 inches to a mile in the early years of the nineteenth century, and their original field survey sheets are preserved in the British Library. They reduced their field sheets to one inch to one mile before the sheets went to the engravers. It is an open question as to whether Bryant had access to these field maps. The evidence of his mapping detail cuts both ways; the outlines of the Broads, for example, appear to be almost identical to those shown by Faden and quite different from those shown by the O.S.[6] However, the detail Bryant shows for Wymondham Park, immediately to the south of Wymondham, is much more in line with that shown by the O.S., the two farm names and the outline of the moat being similar.

i

Faden and Bryant however both note the outlying hamlet of Wymondham as Sinfield; the O.S. show it correctly as Silfield.

An examination of the columns of the *Norfolk Chronicle* and the *Norwich Mercury* for 1826 and early 1827 has proved disappointing in terms of finding further information as to how Bryant might have advertised and publicised his map. No mention occurs in December 1826, yet Longman's published a full list of their new titles. In February 1827 a full list of books issued by the Norwich publishers Bacon and Kinnebrooks appeared, but no notice, article or review of the new map was given.

Analysis of Bryant's Map

The Key and Symbols

Bryant usefully shows the hundred boundaries, a reminder that before the Poor Law was reformed in 1834 the hundred was the nation's administrative unit below that of the county. Ironically, in view of recent decisions by the O.S., Bryant provided parish boundaries too. These were not shown by Faden in 1797 or by the O.S. in 1836-7. As many modern parishes represent a merger of medieval parishes (Reepham for example), it is valuable to have parish boundaries shown as they were 170 years ago.

Gentlemen's seats are shown; these were presumably occupied by subscribers actual or hoped-for. Even the O.S., although not dependent on subscribers, sent sections of their draft maps to landowners for checking.[7]

Skelton in a valuable appendix to his article on the origins of the O.S. gives a set of 'General Instructions for the Officers of the Engineers employed in surveying' the coast and districts of the country near it.[8]

'They will [of course] proceed around the contours and creeks of the shore; along the great roads and lanes and also along the courses of the rivers... The boundaries of Forests, Woods, Heaths, Commons or Morasses... and in the enclosed parts of the Country all the hedges and other Boundaries of Fields are to be carefully laid down... The risings or irregularities of the ground are everywhere to be expressed with care...'

Bryant's key includes all these elements and his scale, slightly larger than Faden's, allowed him to show turnpikes and main roads, good cross and driving roads and lanes and bridleways. The distinction between road capacities would clearly have military value, but it is not always easy to distinguish them on the printed map. Toll bars were also shown, as were fox 'covers', of interest to subscribing gentry no doubt.

Bryant shows settlements more clearly than Faden. This is an advantage of the larger scale, but it does look as if more care was taken to map the layout of buildings than was taken by Faden. Many inn names are given. Bryant, like Faden, shows industrial features such as mills and brickyards. The first edition of the O.S. also shows many sandpits and one wonders whether the Engineers were especially concerned to locate potential road-repair material in case of large-scale military use of roads.

The 'risings or irregularities' of the ground were to pose a major problem for cartographers until contour mapping was introduced by the O.S. in the northern sheets of their first edition from 1847, and in colour from the 1890s.[9] Faden showed relief by means of hachures and often gave an impression of canyon-like relief - most inappropriate to Norfolk.[10] Bryant used a subtler system of hachuring but it is most uneven in its use; for example he shows a slope along the Cawston/Salle parish boundary, on what is a very modest valley, but no hachuring is shown between Worthing and Norwich along the slopes of the Wensum Valley, for example at Ringland Hills. Nearer the coast, the south east peninsula of the county, east of Langley out to Hardley overlooking the marshes, is shown more strongly than by Faden or the O.S. Both Bryant and Faden show the Poringland 'table mountain' in an exaggerated form. When shown, Bryant's representation of relief is subtler than Faden's, but the O.S. first edition is a great improvement on both.

The Broads
Broads change their outline relatively quickly as vegetation clogs them. Bryant's broads outlines are very similar to those of Faden, but by 1837 the O.S. show considerable changes to a number of them. There are differences in names though some, such as Neatisham for Neatishead, are obvious mistakes. Bryant names more inns than Faden; he shows the Chequers Inn at St Benet's Abbey for example. Winmere Hall in Hickling is shown by Bryant as Wigmore Farm. The modern coast road, the B1159, and the Acle Straight, from Acle to Yarmouth, had still not been built.

Williamson in his recent study of the Norfolk Broads notes that Bryant's map showed 73 drainage mills in Broadland as compared with 47 shown by Faden. He raises some doubt as to whether Bryant had recorded all of them, but this is an excellent illustration of the value of these two maps in assessing landscape changes.[11]

The Fens
Parliamentary Enclosure, for example at Feltwell in 1813, resulted in many new drains being cut between the Great Ouse and the New Bedford River. Poppylots Farm at the west edge of Feltwell Common was laid out with an intricate grid system of shelter belts, most unusual for the Fens, and Methwold Common, a featureless area on Faden's map, showed new drains and some shelter belts by 1826. A major feature is the New Cut or Eau Brink that realigned the course of the Great Ouse to the south of King's Lynn. The Sutton Bridge causeway and new bridge were noted as 'planned'

(the Act was passed in 1827). The impact of the first steam drainage pumps is shown by the Modney Hall Farm steam drainage engine which has replaced the three windmills shown by Faden.

The Coast
Much of the detail shown by Bryant on the North Norfolk coast seems to echo that of Faden, but some names are different, Scalds Head for Scolt Head for example. Bryant's mapping of the creeks across the marshes is much more detailed than that of Faden. In Wells two kilns and a marlpit are recorded by Bryant and not by Faden; such differences may represent real changes in industrial activity, reflecting perhaps the greater use of lime in the improved agriculture of the period.

Breckland
Considerable stretches of the brecks were still sheep walks and heaths in 1826, but enclosure had also made an impact here. To the north of Kilverstone, for example, the common field, noted by Faden, has been replaced by a series of shelter belts, probably of Scots pine, as shown by Bryant. A number of Breckland parks had also been extended or elaborated by 1826.

The Valleys and Plateaux of Central Norfolk
The overall impression of central Norfolk as shown on Bryant's map is of a less detailed, or perhaps less 'fussy', map than Faden's. This stems first from the less dominant hachuring and indeed some lack of it entirely. Secondly, as a result of enclosure, much common land on the valley floors, shaded by Faden, has gone and indeed many other commons have also disappeared. This contrast is perhaps the most striking difference between the Norfolk landscape of Faden and that recorded by Bryant. By 1826 most of the new roads had been laid out, new hedges would be established and many new

farms set up on enclosed lands. For example, in the Wattlefield division of Wymondham, a number of houses are shown on the former extensive commons. However, some commons still remained; Plumstead Heath and Barningham Heath to the south of Holt were still open. Some former heaths, such as that of Cawston, were shown by Bryant in the wrong positions.

The differences between Faden and Bryant raise many questions that can lead to further enquiry. Faden shows Godwick Hall, an early Coke house, as extant: Bryant shows it in ruins - only documentary research can reveal whether the maps are right, but at least they raise the question. Worthing church is marked as a ruin on Faden and as an existing church on Bryant - is this an example of Early nineteenth century restoration? Ancient woods are an important element of the landscape and Bryant shows Swinnow or Hockering Wood as alternative names whereas Faden shows them as distinct areas of woodland. Bryant, like other large-scale maps, leads the researcher to further investigations.

Historic Features

There is little consistency shown by Bryant in the portrayal of historic sites. Blackborough Priory is recorded as Blackberry Abbey; Pentney Priory is shown, but Wormegay is not. Wormegay Castle is not distinguished clearly either. The responsibility to record ancient monuments, later accepted by the O.S., had not yet been considered.

The Value of Bryant's Map

David Smith in *Maps and Plans* notes that Bryant's map of the East Riding of Yorkshire is 'one of a handful of maps judged outstanding for accuracy, content and reliability being clearly based on some form of field survey'.[12] Chubb in his account of Norfolk maps describes Bryant's map as 'a splendid map'. Despite the absence of any town plans, it certainly is a valuable link between Faden's first attempt at a one-inch map and the more authoritative O.S. first edition. The slightly larger scale than both Faden and the O.S. allows more detail to be given of buildings, function of buildings and a hierarchy of roads as well as more road names. It provides a very valuable record of the progress of enclosure with new straight roads, straightened watercourses and new drains in the Fens and the Broadland valleys. Finally, the mapping of parish boundaries and the boundaries of the hundreds combine with the many other details discussed to make it a valuable tool and resource for all those interested in the changing landscape of Norfolk.

J.C.Barringer

NOTES
1. Barringer, J.C. (Introduction) Reprinted by Norfolk Record Society Vol. XLII 1975 in six sheets, and 1989 Larks Press in a book of 32 maps with 3 town plans.
2. Harley, J.B. Commentary on O.S. 1st Edition Sheet 38 Cromer. Reprinted 1970 & 1982. David & Charles.
3. Harley, J.B. in Discussion following a paper by Skelton, R.A. 'The Origins of the Ordnance Survey in Great Britain'. *Geographical Journal* Vol. CXXVIII Dec. 1962 p. 428.
4. Chambers, B. 'M.J. Armstrong in Norfolk: the Progress of an Eighteenth Century County Survey'. *Geographical Journal* Vol. CXXX Sept. 1964 427-431. Attention was drawn to this paper by Steve Snelling of the E.D.P.
5. Royal Geographical Society Map Room sheets RGS 3.c2 and RGS 3.c1.
6. Frostick, R. in personal note.
7. Harley, J.B., in introduction to the 1969 David & Charles reprint.
8. Skelton, R.A. Appendix to 'The Origins of the Ordnance Survey of Great Britain' *Geographical Journal* Vol. CXXVIII Pt 4 December 1962 pp.424-6.
9. Hindle, P. *Maps for Local History* Batsford 1988 p. 126.
10. Barringer, J.C. as above p. 7.
11. Williamson, T. *The Norfolk Broads: a Landscape History* M.U.P. 1997 p.118.
12. Smith, D. *Maps and Plans for the Local Historian and Collector.* Batsford 1988 p.80.

Map
OF
THE COUNTY OF
NORFOLK,
FROM Actual Survey
A. BRYANT,
In the Years 1824, 1825, and 1826.
Respectfully Dedicated to the
NOBILITY, CLERGY & GENTRY, OF THE COUNTY,
Published by
A. Bryant, 27, Great Ormond Street, London.

KEY

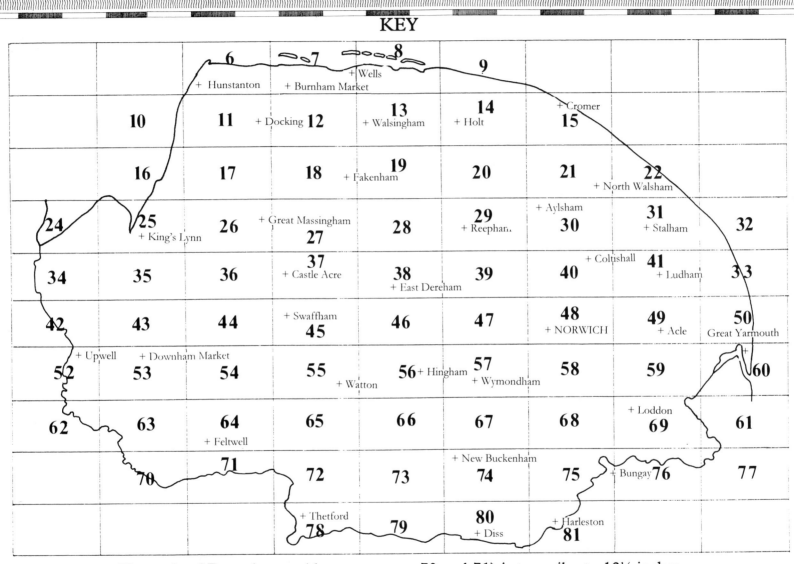

6	7	8 +Wells	9			
+ Hunstanton	+ Burnham Market					
10	11 + Docking 12	13 + Walsingham	14 + Holt	15 +Cromer		
16	17	18 19 + Fakenham	20	21	22 + North Walsham	
24	25 + King's Lynn 26	+ Great Massingham 27	28	29 + Reepham + Aylsham 30	31 + Stalham	32
34	35 36	37 + Castle Acre	38 + East Dereham 39	40	+ Coltishall 41 + Ludham	33
42	43 44	+ Swaffham 45	46	47	48 + NORWICH	49 + Acle 50 Great Yarmouth
52	+ Upwell + Downham Market 53 54	55 + Watton	56 + Hingham 57 + Wymondham	58	59	60
62	63 64 + Feltwell	65	66	67	68 + Loddon 69	61
70	71	72	73	+ New Buckenham 74	75 + Bungay 76	77
	+ Thetford 78	79	80 + Diss	+ Harleston 81		

The scale of Bryant's map (shown on pages 70 and 71) is ten miles to 12¼ inches.

EXPLANATION

Names of Hundreds	as GRIMSHOE
Market Towns	SWAFFHAM
Parishes	Denver
Villages, Gentlemens Seats, Lanes, Heaths,	
Commons, Woods, Hills, Water &c.	In Italics
Buildings	
Churches	
Parks	

Castles

Nursery Grounds & Gardens

Wind & Water Mills

Rivers & Water

Canals

Heaths & Commons

Woods

Hills

Turnpike & Mail Roads

Good Crofs or Driving Roads

Lanes & Bridle Ways

Miles distant from London

Toll Bars

Fox Covers

County Boundary

Hundred Boundary

Parish Boundary

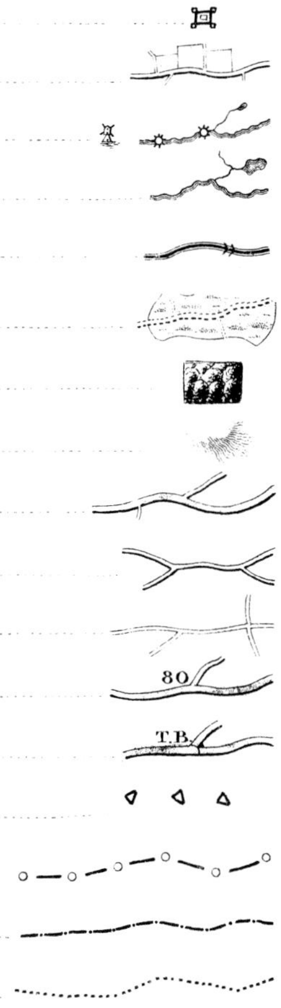

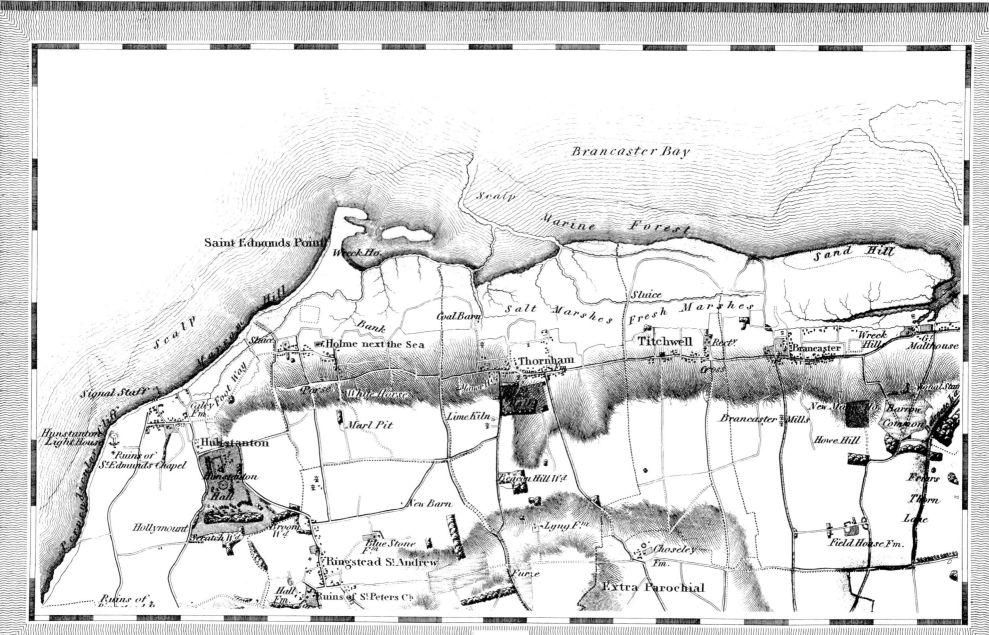

Brancaster Bay

Scalp

Marine Forest

Sand Hill

Saint Edmunds Point

Wreck Ho.

Scalp Hill

Scalp

Coal Barn

Salt Marshes

Sluice

Fresh Marshes

Bank

Holme next the Sea

Titchwell

Rect.y

Wreck Hill

Gt. Malthouse

Brancaster

Shoe

Thornham

Cross

Harrow Foot Way

Signal Staff

White House

Signal Stat.

Caley Foot Way

Hunstanton Cliff

New Malt Ho.

Calcy Fm.

Marl Pit

Lime Kiln

Brancaster Mills

Barron Common

Hunstanton Light House

Hunstanton

Howe Hill

Ruins of St Edmunds Chapel

Hunstanton Hall

Beacon Hill Wd.

Friars

Thorn Lane

Hollymount

New Barn

Lyng Fm.

Scratch Wd.

Broom Wd.

Blue Stone Fm.

Choseley Fm.

Field House Fm.

Ringstead St Andrew

Extra Parochial

Furze

Ruins of

Hall Fm.

Ruins of St Peters Ch.

6

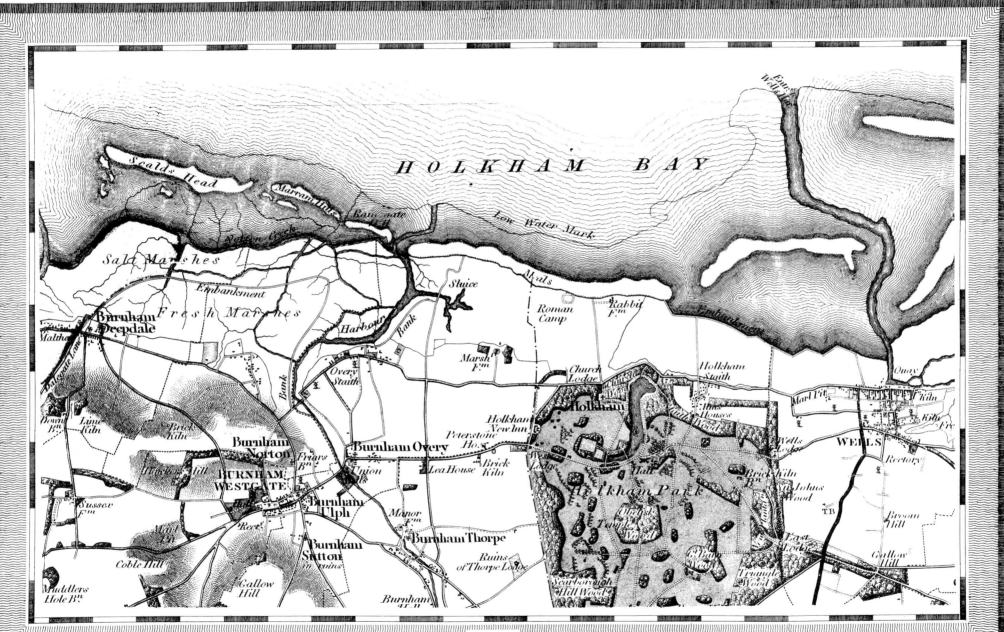

HOLKHAM BAY

Scaldy Head

Marram Hills

Ram Ride

Nelson Creek

Low Water Mark

Salt Marshes

Embankment

Fresh Marshes

Sluice

Marls

Bank

Harbour

Roman Camp

Rabbit F.m

Embankment

Burnham Deepdale

Malthe

Overy Staith

Marsh F.m

Church Lodge

Holkham Staith

Quay

Down B.n

Lime Kiln

Brick Kiln

Holkham

Marl Pit

Kiln

Holkham New Inn

Peterstone Ho.

Wood

Ice Houses

Wells Lodge

Kiln

Burnham Norton

Friars B.n

Burnham Overy

West Lodge

Hall

Brick Kiln B.n

WELLS

Rectory

Brock Hill

BURNHAM WESTGATE

Union

Lea House

Brick Kiln

Holkham Park

St Johns Wood

Sussex F.m

Manor F.m

Obelisk Temple Wood

Broom Hill

Burnham Ulph

East Lodge

Rec.t

Coble Hill

Burnham Sutton

Ruins

Burnham Thorpe

Ruins of Thorpe Lodge

Gd Barn Wood

Gallow Hill

Muddlers Hole B.n

Gallow Hill

Burnham H.m

Scarborough Hill Wood

Triangle Wood

7

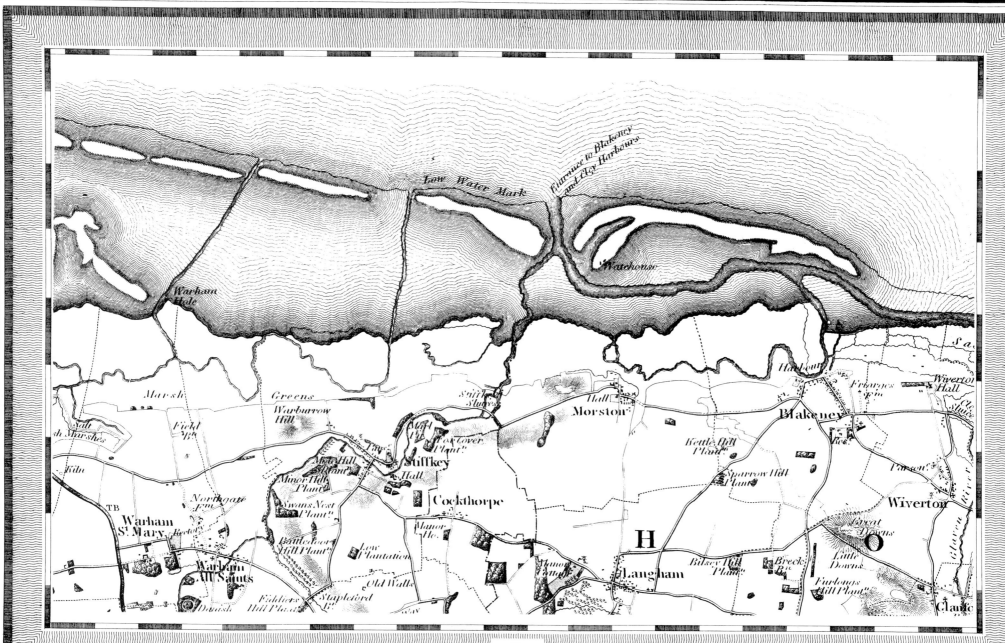

Low Water Mark

Entrance to Blakeney and Cley Harbours

Watchouse

Warham Hole

Marsh

Greens

Warburrow Hill

Salt Sluices

Morston

Hall

Blakeney

Friarges Fm

Wiverton Hall

Salt Marshes

Salt

Field Bn

Mill Hill

Foxcover Plant.

Kettle Hill Plant.

Kiln

Mill Hill Plant.

Minor Hill Plant.

Stiffkey

Hall

Sparrow Hill Plant.

Parson?

Northgate Fm

TB

Warham St Mary

Rectory

Swans Nest Plant.

Cockthorpe

Manor Ho.

Wiverton

Great Downs

H

O

Warham All Saints

Bottletoor Hill Plant.

Low Plantation

Manor Cottage

Langham

Bilsey Hill Plant.

Breck Bn

Little Downs

Fiddlers Hill Plant.

Stapleford Ln

Old Walls

Way

Manor Cottage

Furlongs Hill Plant.

Danish

Way

Clare?

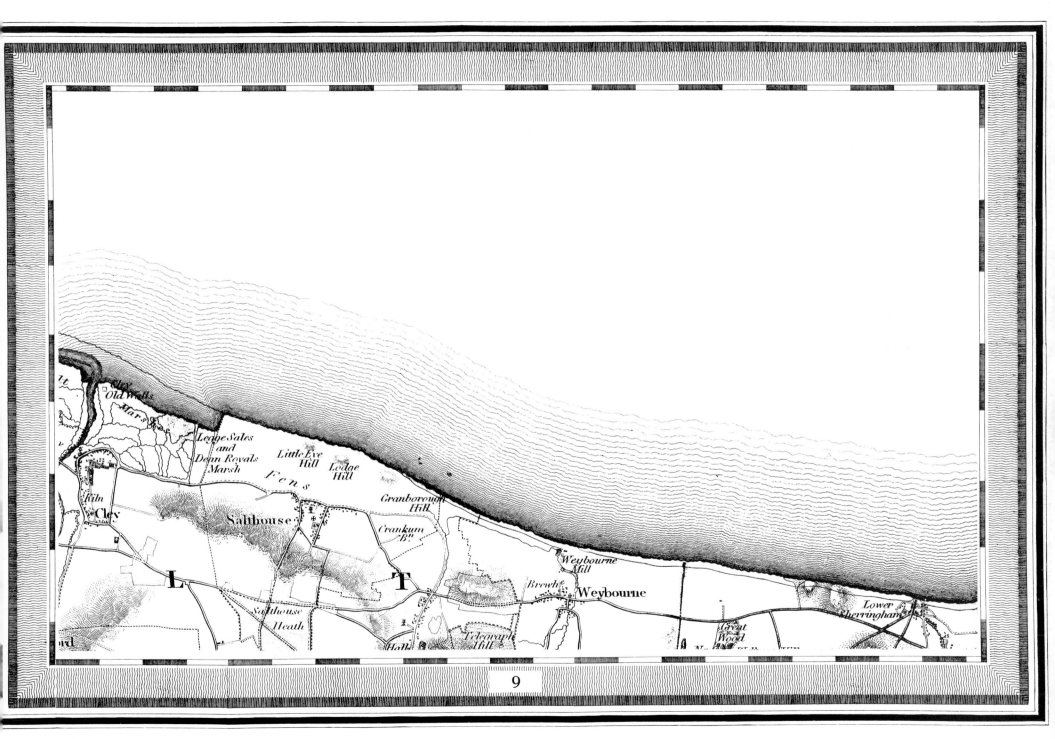

Old Walls

Old Walls

Marsh

Legge Sales
and
Denn Royals
Marsh

Little Eve
Hill

Lodge
Hill

Fens

Granborough
Hill

Kiln

Cley

Salthouse

Crankum
B"

Weybourne
Mill

L   T   Brewhe   Weybourne

Salthouse
Heath

Great
Wood

Lower
Sherringham

Holt   Telegraph
Hill

9

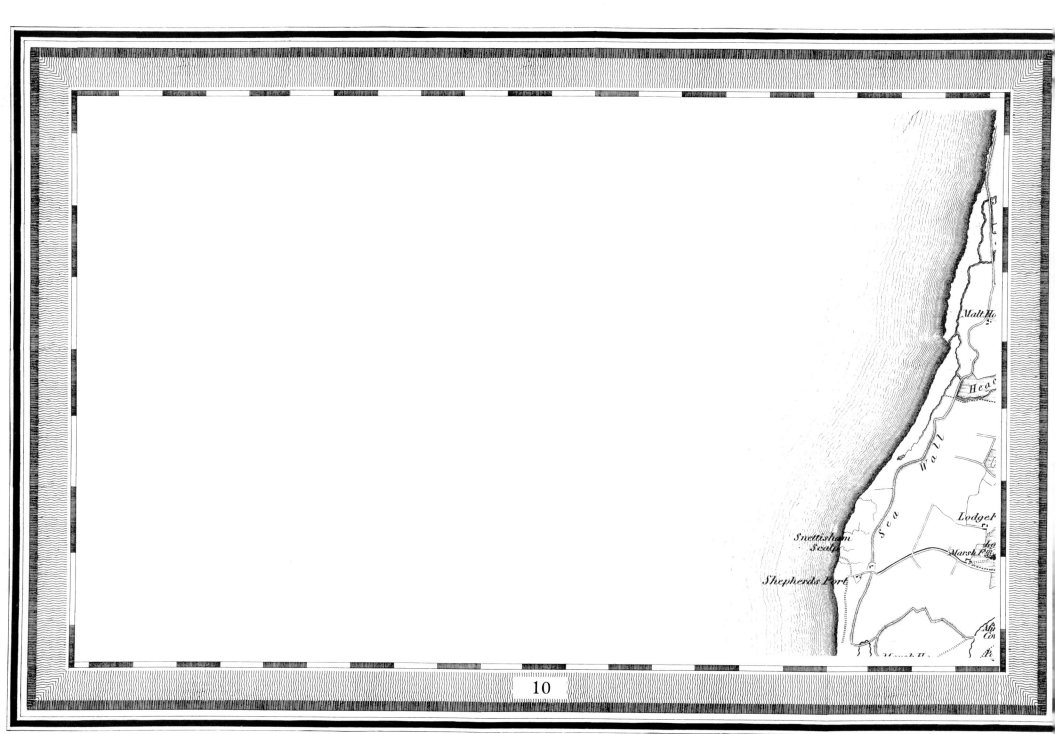

Malt Ho

Hea

Sea Wall

Lodge

Snettisham
Scale

Marsh F

Shepherds Port

Ma
Co

Marsh H

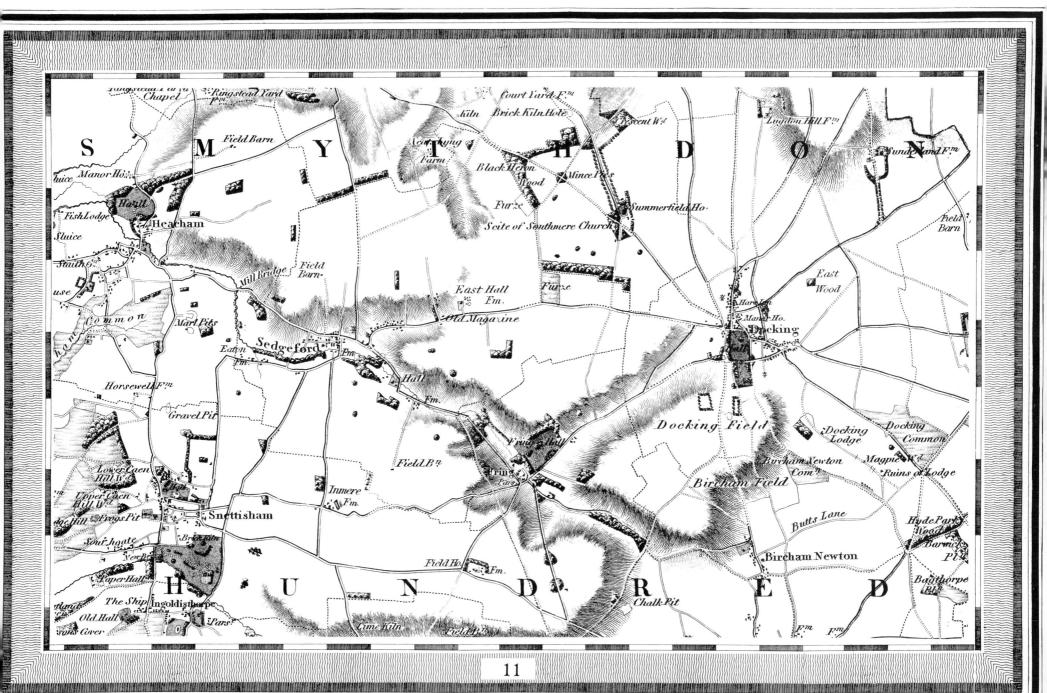

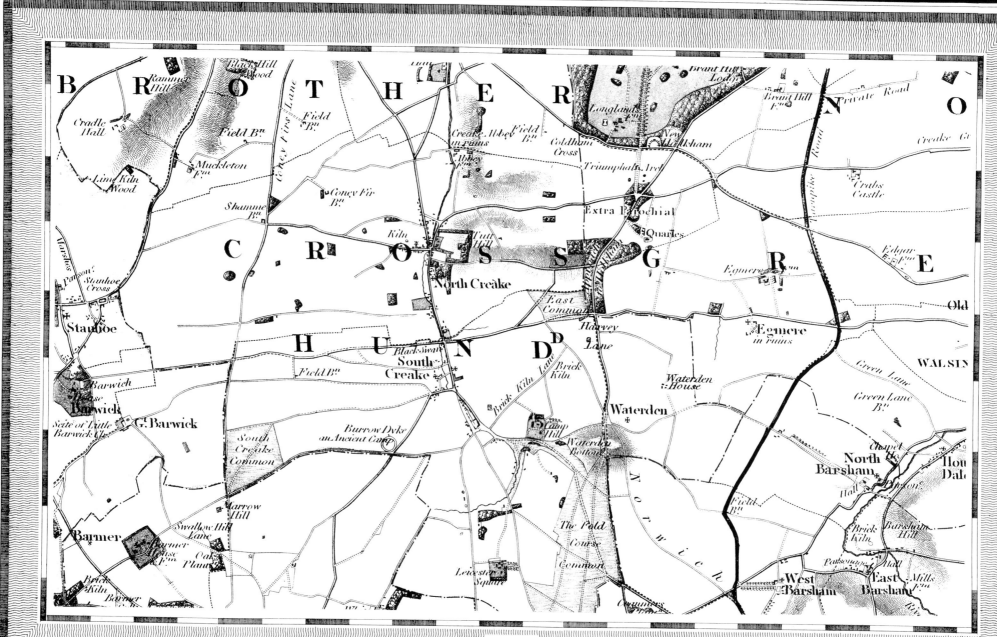

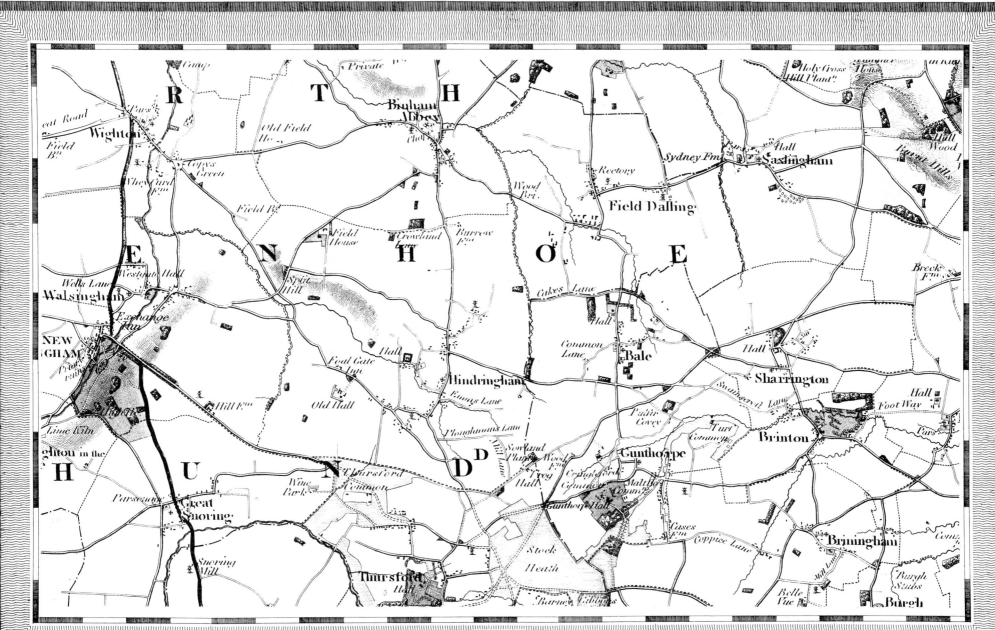

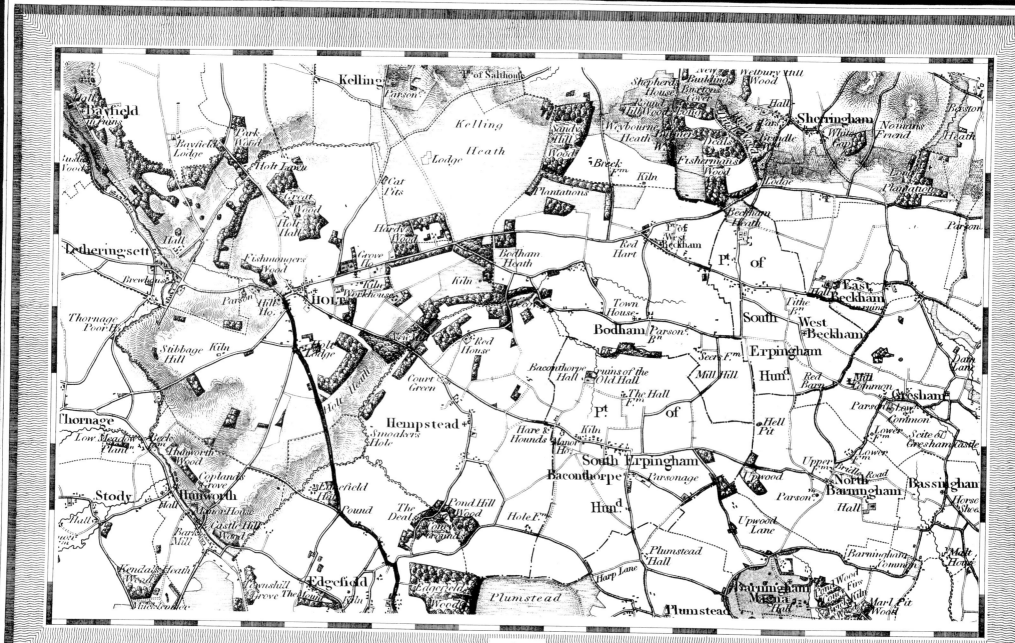

Holt in ruins

Bayfield

Bayfield Lodge

Park Wood

Kelling

P^t of Salthouse

Kelling Heath

Lodge

Sandy Hill Wood

Shepherds House
Round Hill Wood
New Building
Ringers Cover
Pond

Welbury Hill Wood

Hall

Sheringham

Beeston Heath

Nonnans Friend

Holt Lawn

Great Wood

Cat Pits

Weybourne Heath

Wood

Brick F^m

Breck F^m

Fishermans Wood

Parson

Kiln

Lodge

Bayston Wood

Lowr Plantation

Letheringsett

Hall

Holt Hall

Hards Wood

Grove Ho

Plantations

Bodham Heath

Red Hart

P^t of West Beckham

Beckham Heath

Parson

Brewhouse

Fishmongers Wood

Kiln

Workhouse

HOLT

Kiln

Kiln

Town House

P^t of South

East Beckham

Tithe Bⁿ

Hall

Thornage Poor Ho

Parson
Hill Ho

New

Red House

Deer

Bodham

Parson Bⁿ

West Beckham

Erpingham

Stibbage Hill

Kiln

Holt Lodge

Holt Heath

Court Green

Baconthorpe Hall

ruins of the Old Hall

The Hall F^m

Seers F^m

Mill Hill

Hun^d

Red Barn

Red Common

Gresham

Parson Low Common

Thornage

Holt Heath

Hempstead

Smoakers Hole

P^t

of

Hell Pit

Lower F^m

Scite of Gresham Castle

Low Meadow Plantⁿ

Beck F^m

Hunworth Wood

Hare & Hounds

Manor Ho

Kiln

South Erpingham

Upper

Bridle Road

Lower F^m

Stody

Coplands Grove

Hunworth Hall

Manor House

Ellesfield Hill

Pound

The Deal

Pond Hill Wood

Baconthorpe

Hun^d

Parsonage

Parson

Upwood

North Barningham

Bassingham

Hall

Hall

Bark Mill

Castle Hill Wood

Hole F^m

Upwood Lane

Horse Shoe

Kendals Heath Wood

Townshill Grove

Edgefield

The Mount

Edgefield Wood

Plumstead

Harp Lane

Plumstead Hall

Barningham Common

Malt House

Whitebridon

Kiln

Barningham Magna

Pond Wood

Long Furs

Marl Pit Wood

Hall

Plumstead

14

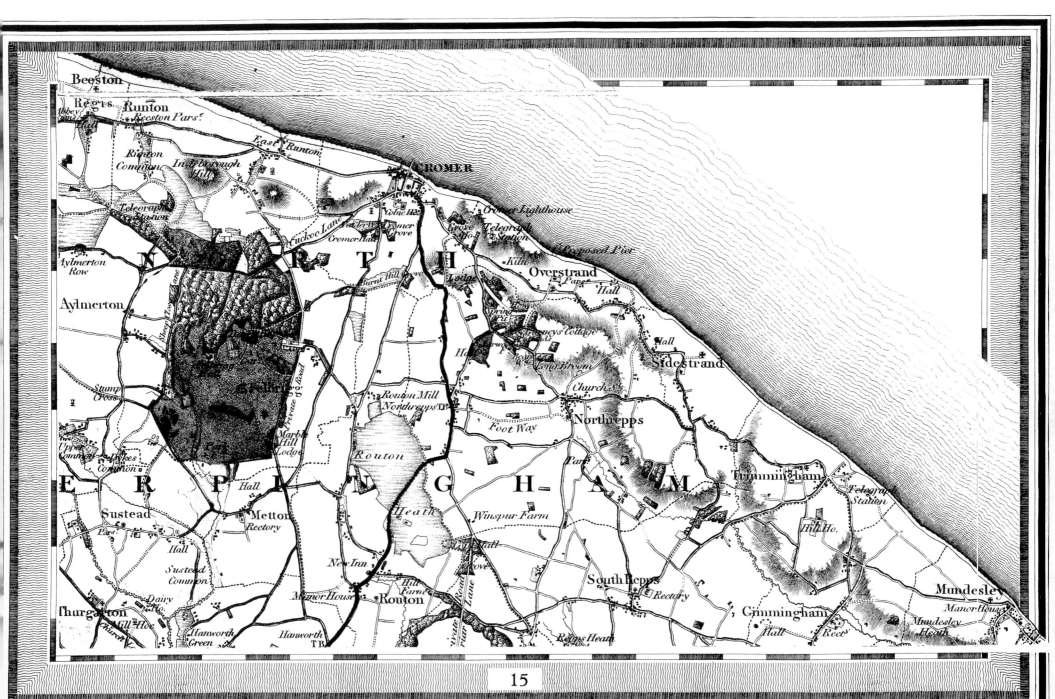

Beeston
Regrs
Runton
Beeston Pars?
East Runton
Runton Common
Inceborough Hill
Telegraph Station
Aylmerton Row
Aylmerton
N   O   R   T   H
Cuckoo Lane
Cromer Hall
Cromer Grove
Colne H?
CROMER
Cromer Lighthouse
Cross H?
Telegraph Station
Proposed Pier
Burnt Hill Grove
Lodge
Overstrand
Paper
Hall
Spring Pit
Gurney's Cottage
Hall
Sidestrand
Sheep Yew Lane
Stump Cross
Private Road
Marble Hill Lodge
Routon Mill
Northrepps
Foot Way
Church S?
Northrepps
Upper Common
Dukes Common
Hall
E   R   P   I   N   G   H   A   M
Routon
Park
Trimmingham
Telegraph Station
Sustead
Metton Rectory
Heath
Winspur Farm
Hill Ho.
Hall
Sustead Common
New Inn
Cross Hall Grove
Hill Farm
South Repps
Rectory
Mundesley
Dairy Ho.
Manor House
Routon
Private Road
Friar Lane
Gimmingham
Manor House
Thurgarton
Mill Ho.
Church
Hanworth Green
Hanworth
T.B.
Repps Heath
Hall
Rect?
Mundesley Heath

15

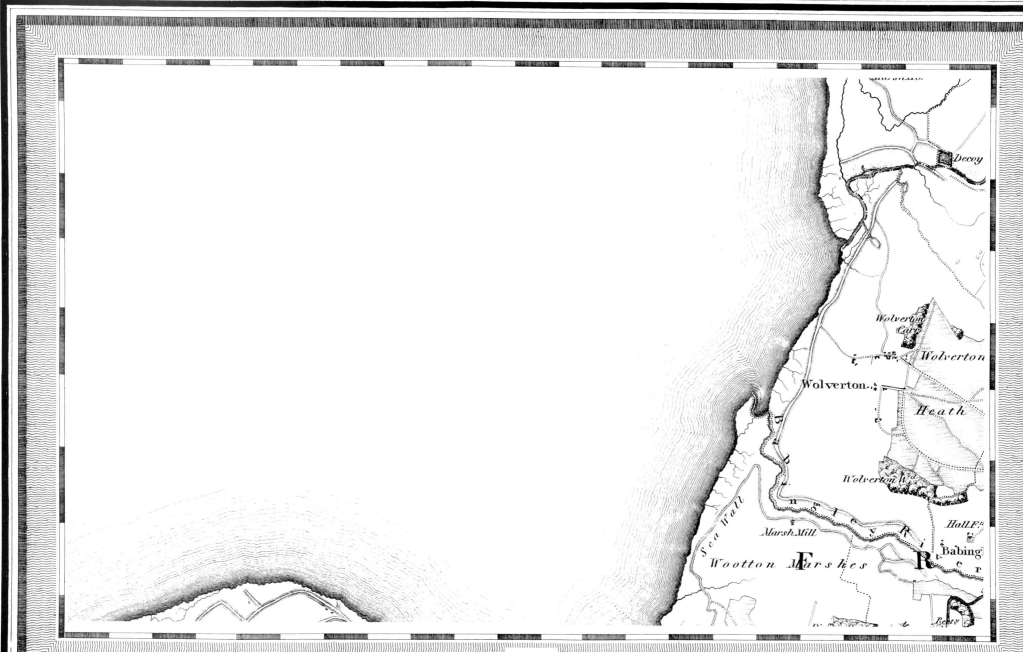

Decoy

Wolverton Carr

Wolverton

Wolverton.

Heath

Wolverton W^d

Sea Wall

Marsh Mill

Hall F^n

Babing

Wootton Marshes

R

Betsy

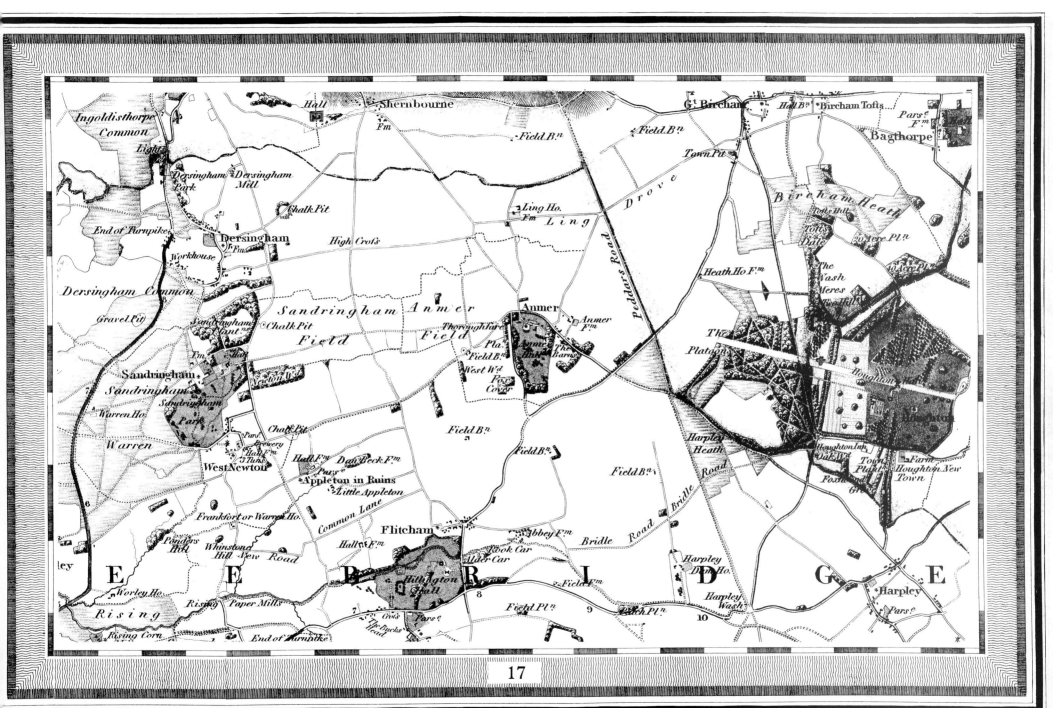

Ingoldisthorpe Common

Light

Dersingham Park   Dersingham Mill

Chalk Pit

End of Turnpike   Dersingham   Fm.

Workhouse

Dersingham Common

Gravel Pit

Sandringham Plant.ns   Chalk Pit

Sandringham   Fm.   Hall

Sandringham

Sandringham   Sandringham

Warren Ho.   Park

Warren

Parr.   Brewery

Hall Fm.   Hall Fm.   Dan Beck Fm.

West Newton   Parr.   Appleton in Ruins

Little Appleton

Frankfort or Warren Ho.   Common Lane

Ponders Hall   Whinstone Hill   New Road

ley

Worley Ho.

Rising   Paper Mills

Rising

Rising Corn

End of Turnpike

Hall   Shernbourne

Fm.

Field B.n   Field B.n

Ling Ho. Fm.   Ling

High Crofs

Sandringham   Anmer   Field   Anmer

Field   Field   Anmer Fm.

Thoroughfare   Anmer Park   The Barns

Pla.   Field B.n

West W.d   Fox Cover

Chalk Pit   Newton W.d

Field B.n

Field B.n

Field B.n

Flitcham

Hall Fm.   Abbey Fm.   Bridle Road   Bridle Road

Rook Car   Field Fm.

E   E   P   Alder Car   R   I   Field

Hillington Hall   8

Crofs   Parr.   Field Pl.n   9

The Bucks Head   Ditch Pl.n   10

G.t Bircham   Hall B.n   Bircham Tofts   Parr. Fm.

Bagthorpe

Town Pit

Bircham Heath

Field B.n   Tofts Hill   20 Acre Pl.n

Tofts Dale

Peddars Road   The Wash Meres

Drove   Heath Ho. Fm.

The Plantations   Houghton

Harpley Heath   Houghton

Harpley   Road   Houghton Inn   Farm

Oak W.d   Town Plant.   Houghton New Town

Foxhole   Grove

D   G   E

Harpley Dam Ho.   Harpley

Harpley Wash   Parr.

17

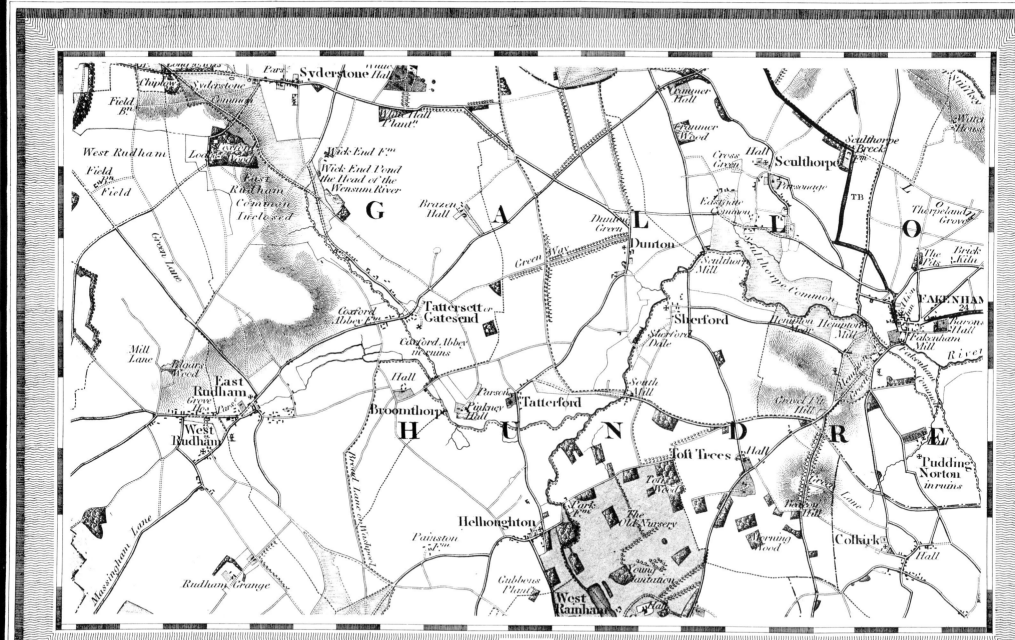

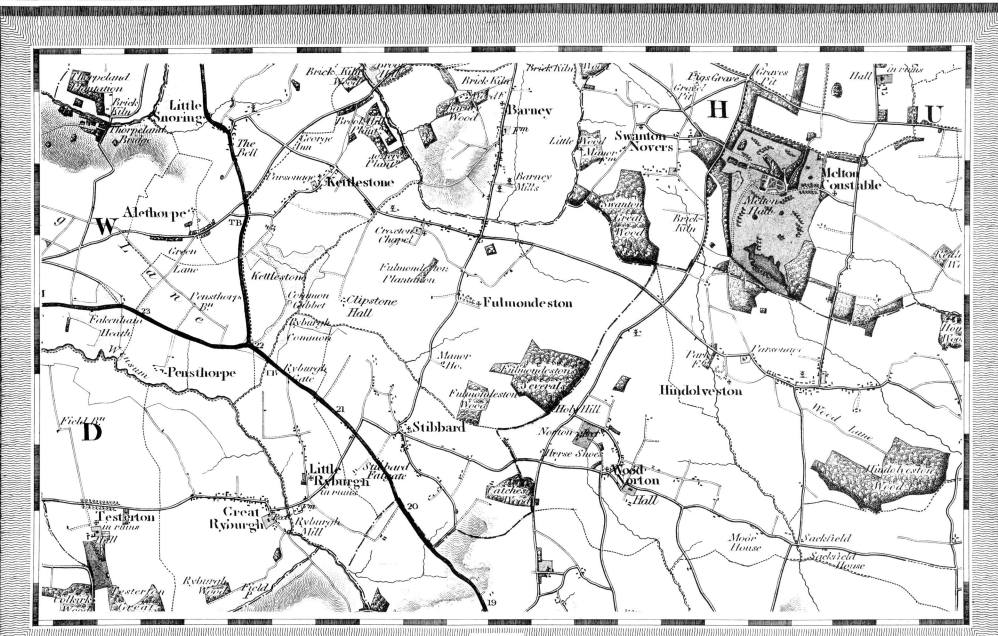

Thorpeland Plantation
Brick Kiln
Little Snoring
Thorpeland Bridge
The Bell
George Inn
Brick Kiln Wood
Brick Kiln Plant.
Brick Kiln
Barney Wood
Barney
Fm
Swanton Novers
Little Wood Manor Fm
Pigs Grave
Graves Pit
Graves Pit
Hall in ruins
H
U
Melton Constable
Parsonage
Kettlestone
Ackery's Plant.
Alethorpe
W
Green Lane
TB
Croxton Chapel
Barney Mills
Swanton Great Wood
Brick Kiln
Melton Hall
Red Wd
Pensthorpe Bn
Kettlestone
Fulmondeston Plantation
Fulmondeston
Hog Wood
Fakenham Heath
23
Wensum
Common Gibbet
Ryburgh
Clipstone Hall
Common
22
Manor Ho.
Fulmondeston Severals
Parsonage
Park Fm
Hindolveston
Pensthorpe
D
Ryburgh Gate
TB
Ryburgh Gate
Fulmondeston Wood
Holt Hill
Norton Street
Wood Lane
Field Bn
21
Stibbard
Horse Shoes
Wood Norton
Hall
Hindolveston Wood
Little Ryburgh
Stibbard Faltgate
in ruins
Catches Wood
Testerton in ruins
Great Ryburgh
Fm
Ryburgh Mill
20
Moor House
Sackfield
Sackfield House
Colkirk Wood
Testerton Great
Ryburgh Wood
Field P.
19

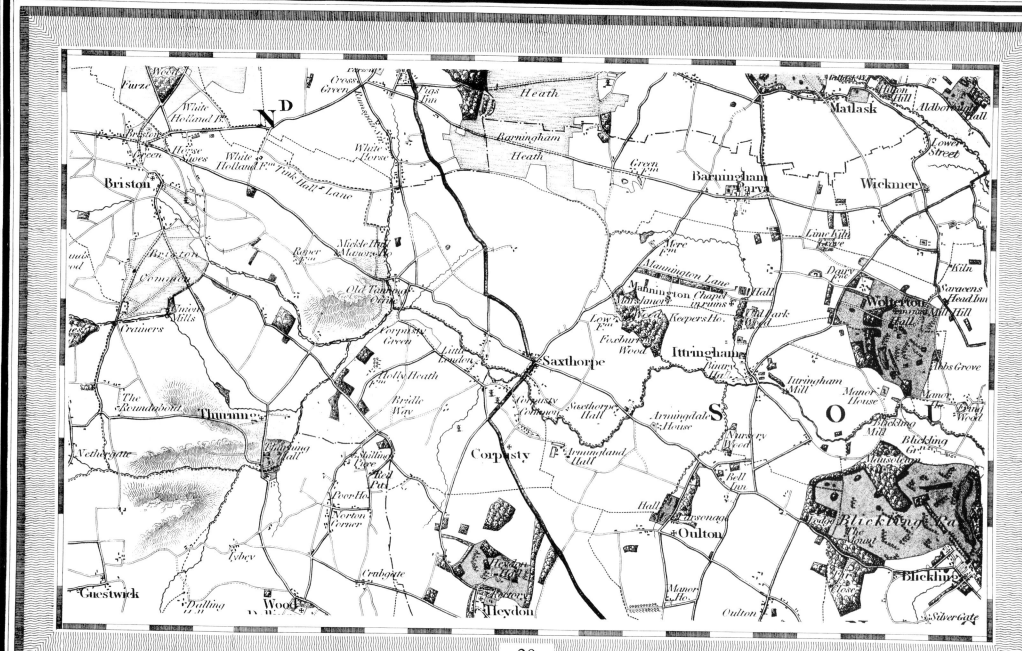

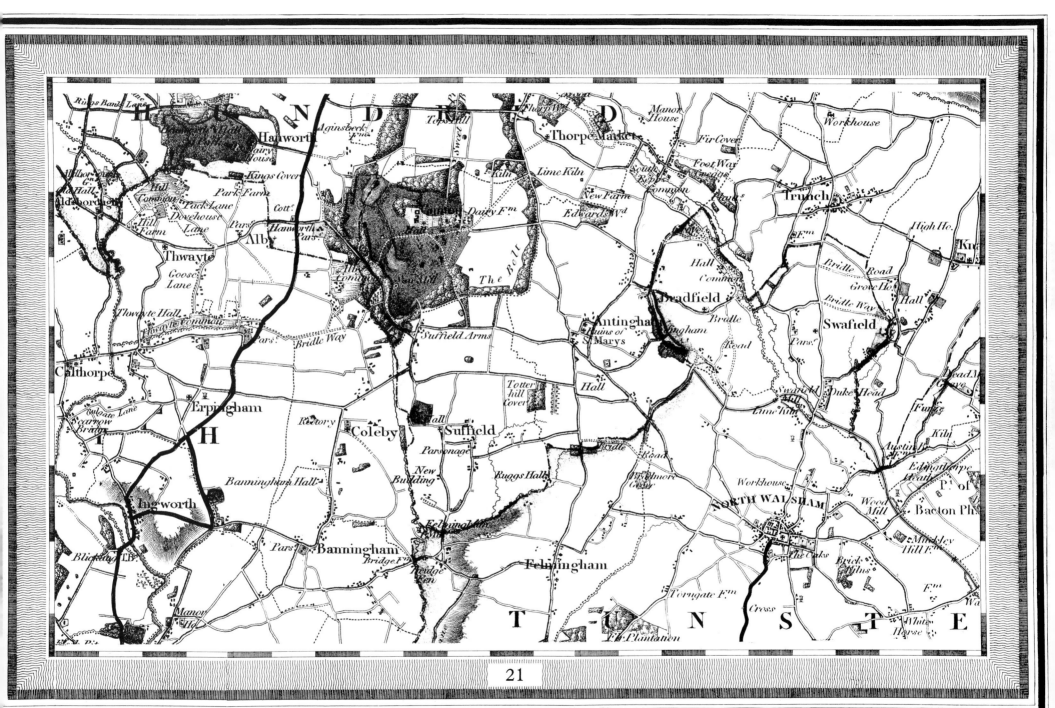

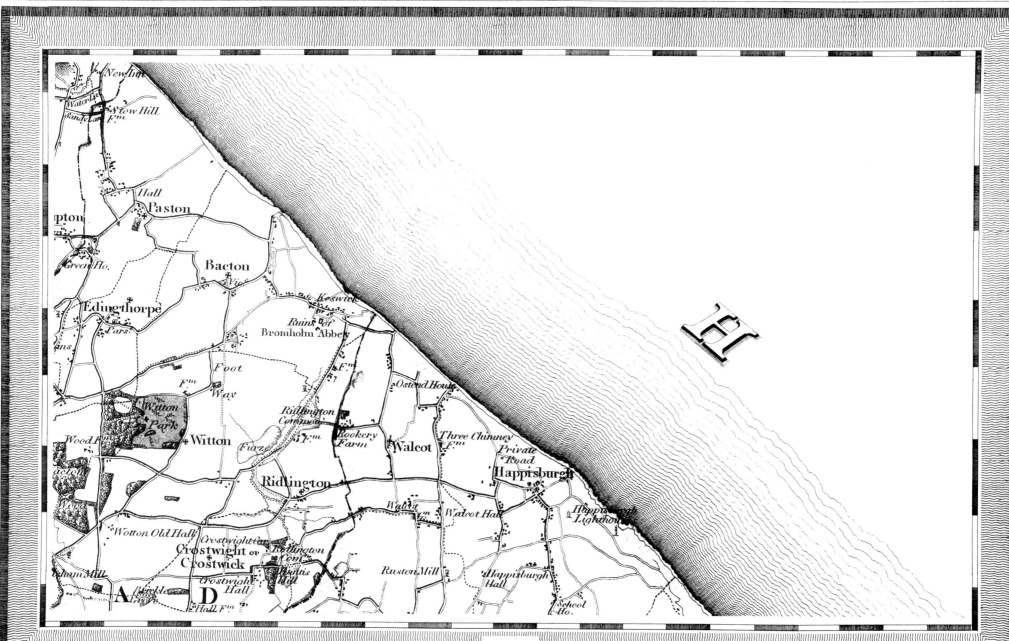

New Inn

Water Pit

Stow Hill

Sandy Lane Fm

Hall

Paston

pton

Green Ho.

Bacton

Vic:

Edingthorpe

Pars

Keswick

Ruins of
Bromholm Abbey

Foot
Way

Fm

Ostend House

Witton
Park

Ridlington
Common

Fm

Three Chimney
Fm

Wood Fm

Witton

Furze

Rookery
Farm

Walcot

Private
Road

Happisburgh

Ridlington

Walcot

Walcot Hall

Happisburgh
Lighthouse

Wotton Old Hall

Crostwight or
Crostwick

Crostwight
Hall

Ridlington
Cem:

Ruston Mill

Happisburgh
Hall

sham Mill

A   D

Curtis
Hall

Crostwight
Hall

School
Ho.

Hall Fm

H

22

Ecclesiastical Divisions

The County of Norfolk is in the Diocese of Norwich (except Emneth) and contains the Archdeaconries of Norwich and Norfolk.

The Archdeaconry of Norwich, comprises the 13 following Deaneries, viz.

The Archdeaconry of Norfolk, includes the 12 Deaneries, of

BLOFIELD Cont.ᵍ the Hundred of BLOFIELD and WALSHAM	**BRECCLES** Cont.ᵍ the Hundred of WAYLAND (except the Parish of Rockland St. Peter)	**BRISLEY** Cont.ᵍ the Hundred of LAUNDITCH (except the Parish of Hoo & the Hamlet of Dilling-ton)	**FLEGG** Cont.ᵍ the Hundreds of EAST & WEST FLEGG	**HOLT** Cont.ᵍ the Hundred of HOLT with the Parishes of Field Dalling & Sherring-ham

BROOKE Cont.ᵍ the Hundreds of CLAVERING HENSTEAD & LODDON	**BURNHAM** Cont.ᵍ the Hundreds of BROTHERCROSS & GALLOW except the Parishes of Helhoughton, Hempton, Pudding Nor-ton, Rainham St. Martin, East & West Rainhams, West Rudham, Shereford, Testerton and Toft Trees.	**CRANWICH** Cont.ᵍ the Hundreds of GRIMSHOE & SOUTH GREENHOE also the Parish of Beechamwell	**DEPWADE** Cont.ᵍ the Hundred of DEPWADE

INGWORTH Cont.ᵍ the Hundred of SOUTH ERPINGHAM	**LYNN** Cont.ᵍ the Hundreds of FREEBRIDGE LYNN and FREEBRIDGE MARSHLAND except the Parish of Emneth	**NORWICH** Containing the City of NORWICH except the Parishes of Eaton Higham & Laken-ham	**SPARHAM** Cont.ᵍ the Hundred of EYNSFORD

FINCHAM Cont.ᵍ the Hundred of CLACKCLOSE except the Parish of Beechamwell	**HINGHAM** Cont.ᵍ the Hundreds of FOREHOE & MITFORD also the Parishes of Hoo & Melton Parva	**HITCHAM** Cont.ᵍ the Hundred of SMYTHDON	**HUMBLEYARD** Cont.ᵍ the Hundred of HUMBLEYARD except the Parish of Melton Parva and also the Pa-rishes of Eaton, Higham and Lakenham.

TAVERHAM Cont.ᵍ the Hundred of TAVERHAM	**THETFORD** Cont.ᵍ the Parishes of St. Cuthbert St. Mary St. Peter } Thetford	**TOFT TREES** Cont.ᵍ the Parishes of Helhoughton, Hempton, Pudding Norton, Rainham St. Martin, East and West Rainhams, West Rudham, Shereford, Testerton and Toft Trees.	**WALSINGHAM** Cont.ᵍ the Hundred of SOUTH GREENHOE except the Parish of Field Dalling

REDENHALL Cont.ᵍ the Hundreds of DISS & EARSHAM	**REPPS** Cont.ᵍ the Hundred of NORTH ERPINGHAM except the Parish of Sherringham	**ROCKLAND** Cont.ᵍ the Hundreds of GUILTCROSS & SHROPHAM also the Parish of Rockland St. Peter	**WAXHAM** Cont.ᵍ the Hundreds of HAPPING & TUNSTEAD

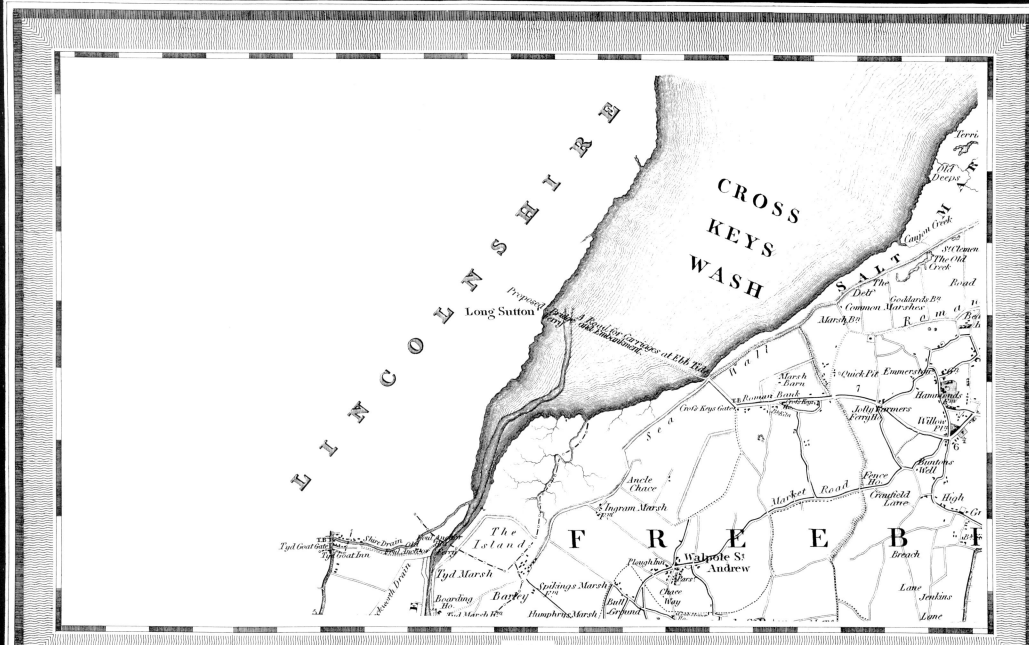

CROSS

KEYS

WASH

LINCOLNSHIRE

Proposed Bridge
Long Sutton &
A Road for Carriages at Ebb Tide
and Embankment.

SALT MA

Old
Deeps

Terri

Canjou Creek

St Clement

The Old
Creek

The
Delf
Common Marshes
Marsh Br

Goddards Br

Road

Roman

Ben

Quick Pit
Emmerston
7
Hammonds Fm

Marsh
Barn

Sea

Wall

Marsh
Barn

Roman Bank
TB

Cross Keys
Br Kiln

Cross Keys Gate

Jolly Farmers
Ferry Ho
Willow
Pit

6

Buntons
Well

Ancle
Chace

Fence
Ho.

Cranfield
Lane

High

Gt

Ingram Marsh
Fm.

Market Road

Tyd Goat Gate
TB
Shire Drain
Foul Anchor
Tyd Goat Inn
Foul Anchor

The
Island

Ferry

F R E E B

Breach

Lane

Walpole St
Andrew

Ploughn

Jenkins
Lane

Tyd Marsh

ockworth Drain

E

Boarding
Ho.
Tyd Marsh Fm

Barley

Spikings Marsh
Fm.

Pars

Bull
Ground

Chace
Way

Humphrys Marsh

24

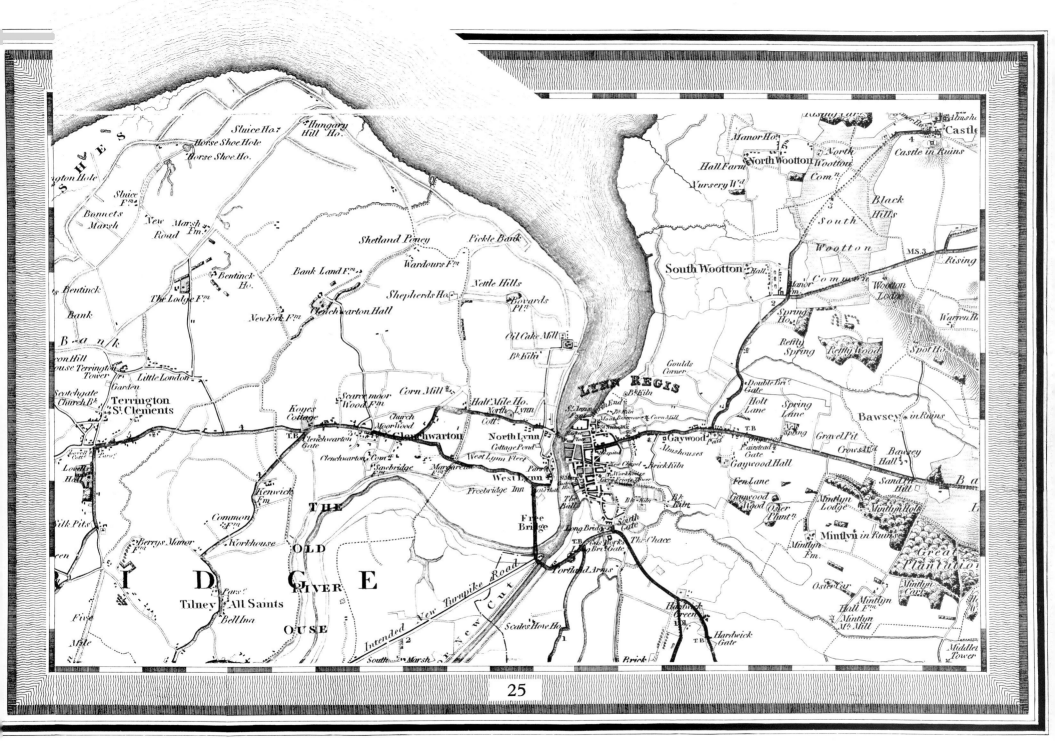

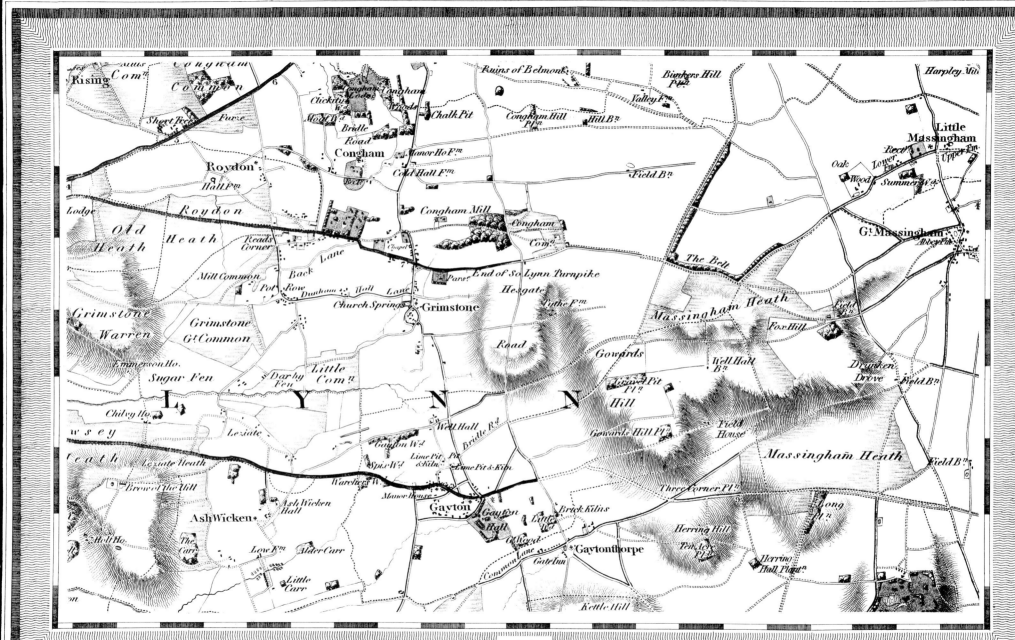

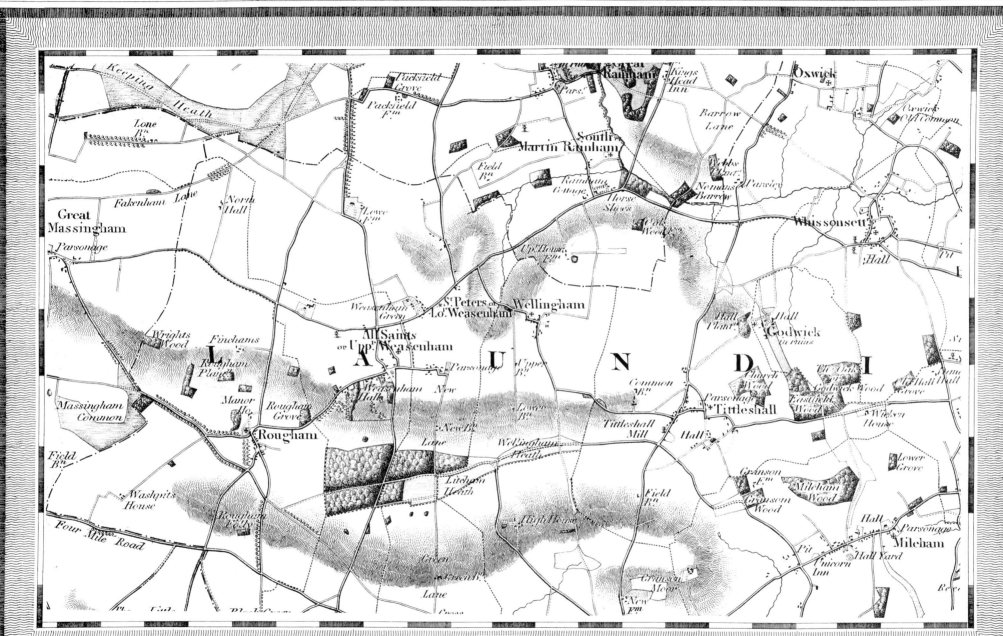

Keeping Heath

Lone Bⁿ

Fakenham Lane

North Hall

Packfield Grove

Packfield F^m

Gt Rainham

Kings Head Inn

Oxwick

Oxwick Old Common

Pars.

South Rainham

Martin Rainham

Barrow Lane

Great Massingham

Parsonage

Lowe F^m

Field Bⁿ

Rainham Cottage

Horse Shoes

Webbs F^{mr}

Nomans Barrow

Parsley

Whissonsett

Hall

Oak Wood

Up^r House F^m

Pit

L A U N D I

Weasenham Green

St Peters or Lo^r Weasenham

Wellingham

Hall F^m

Hall

Godwick in ruins

Wrights Wood

Finchams

All Saints or Upp^r Weasenham

Parsonage

Upper Bⁿ

Church Wood

The Oak

Godwick Wood

Hall Hall Grove

Roughan Plan

Manor Ho.

Rougham Grove

Weasenham Hall

New

Common Bⁿ

Parsonage

Eastfield Wood

Tittleshall

Welson House

Massingham Common

Rougham

New Bⁿ

Lower Bⁿ

Lane

Wellingham Heath

Tittleshall Mill

Hall

Lower Grove

Field Bⁿ

Field Bⁿ

Litcham Heath

Granson F^m

Granson Wood

Mileham Wood

Washpits House

High House

Hall

Parsonage

Four Mile Road

Rougham Heath

Green

Granson Moor

Pit

Hall Yard

Mileham

Unicorn Inn

Lane

New F^m

Black Green

Lane

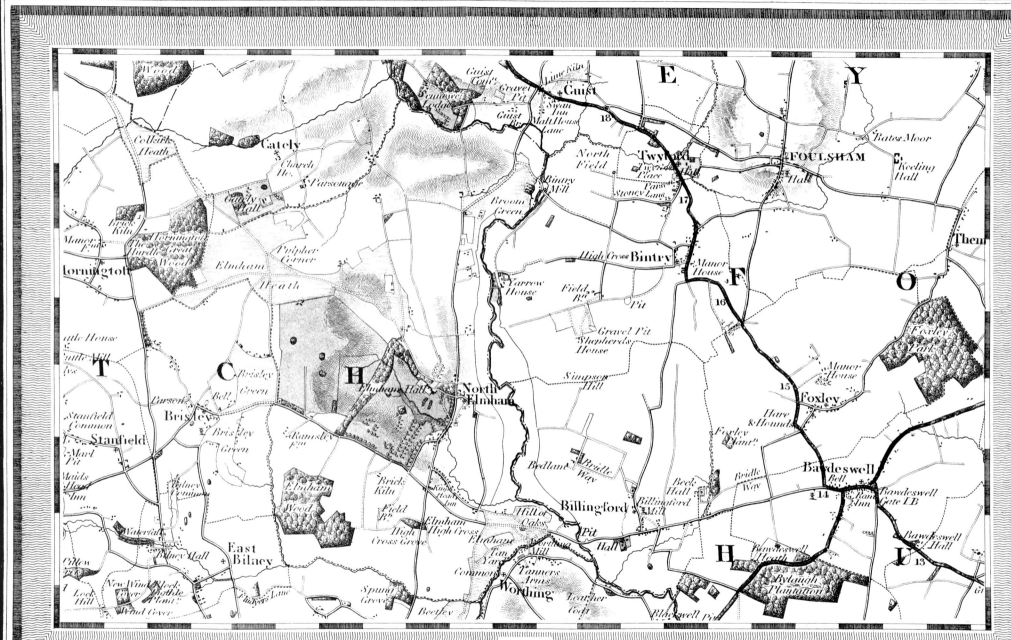

28

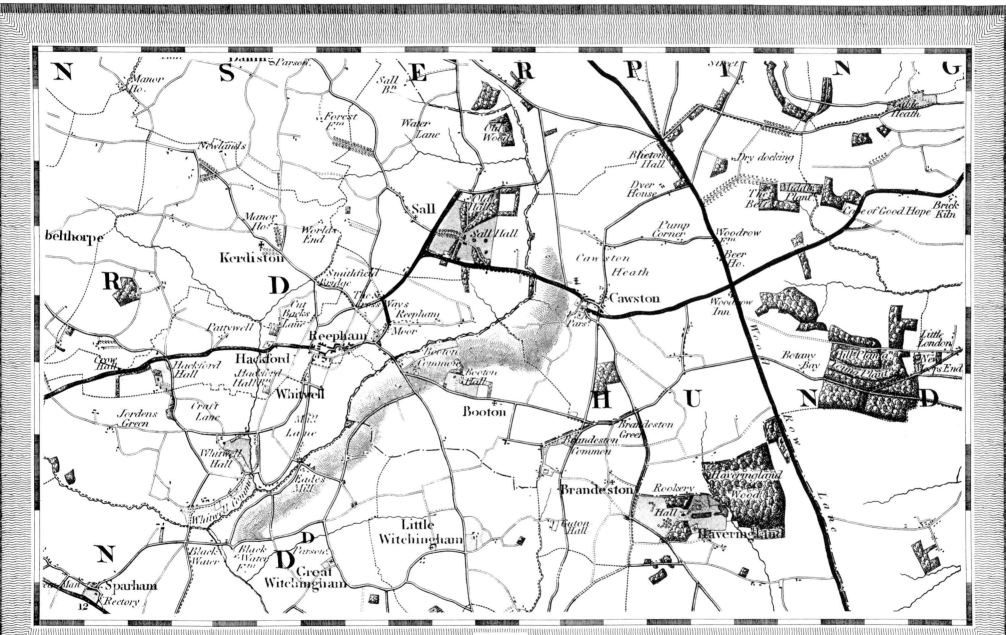

N   S   E   R   P   T   N   G

Manor Ho.

Darling   Parson.

Sall Br.

Forest Fm.

Water Lane

Old Wood

Newlands

Blieton Hall

Dry docking

Street

Little Heath

Sall

Old Hall

Manor Ho.

Worlds End

Sall Hall

Dyer House

Pump Corner

Woodrow Fm.

The Bell

Middle Plant

Cape of Good Hope

Brick Kiln

belthorpe

Kerdiston

Smithfield Bridge

Cawston Heath

Beer Ho.

R

D

The S.

Cut Backs Lane

Ways Reepham

Cawston

Woodrow Inn

Pattywell

Moor

Pars.

Hill Plant &

Botany Bay

Little London

Crow Hall

Hackford Hall

Reepham

Beeton Common

Large Plant

Ways End

Hackford

Hackford Hall Br.

Booton Hall

H   U   N   D

Jordens Green

Whitwell

Croft Lane

Booton

Brandeston Green

Haveringland Wood

Whitwell Hall

M.? Lane

Brandeston Common

Rookery

Eades Mill

Brandeston

Hall

Haveringland

Whitwell Common

D

Little Witchingham

Buxton Hall

N

Black Water

Black Water Fm.

Parson.

Great Witchingham

D

Sparham

Rectory

12

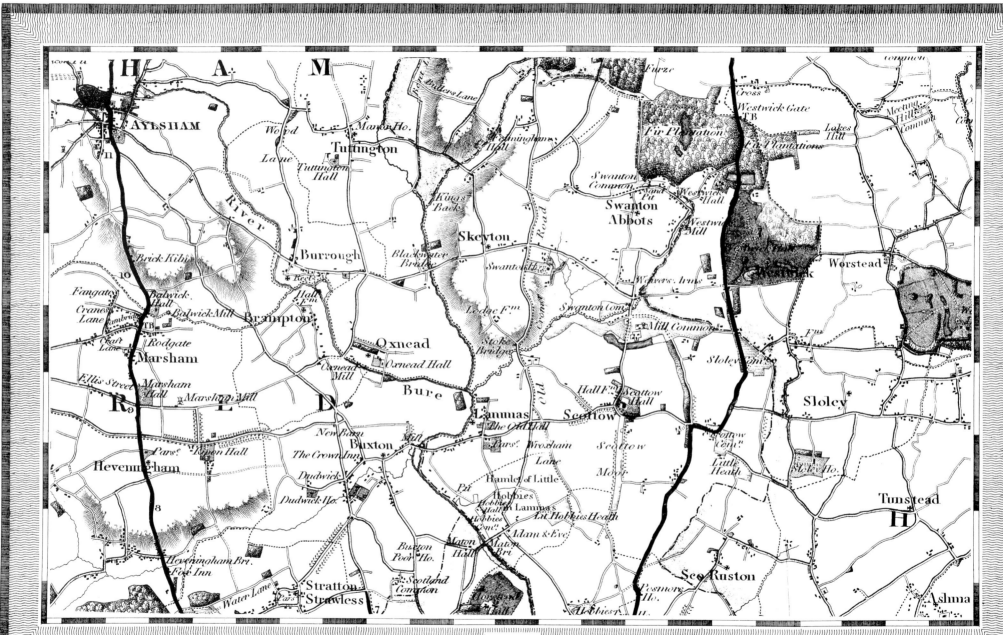

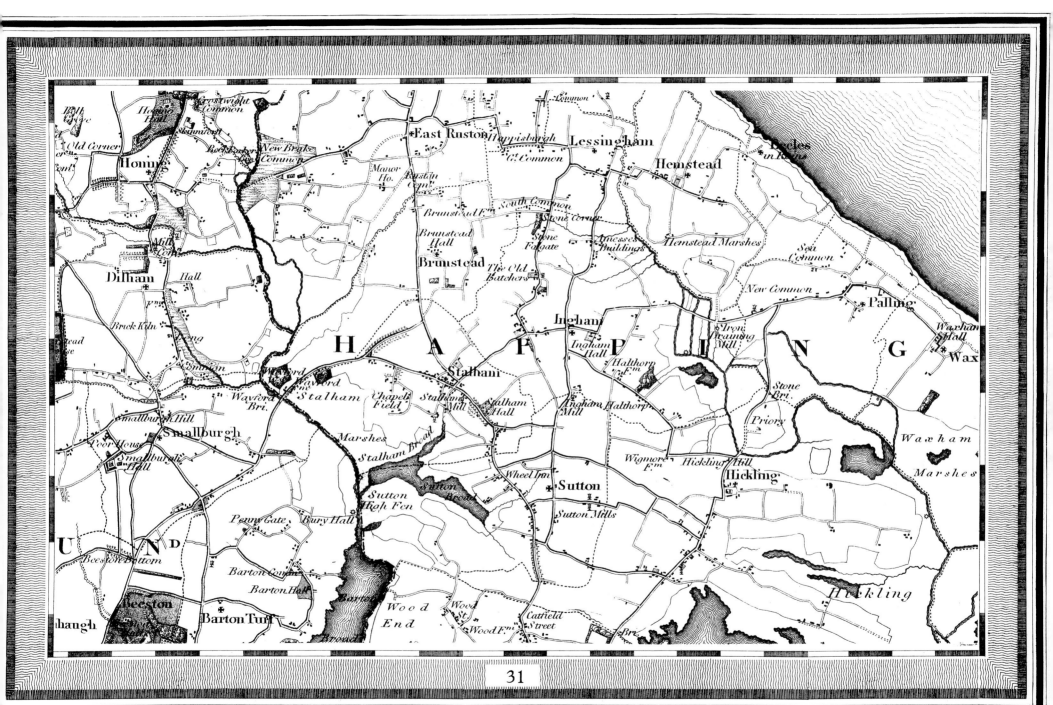

31

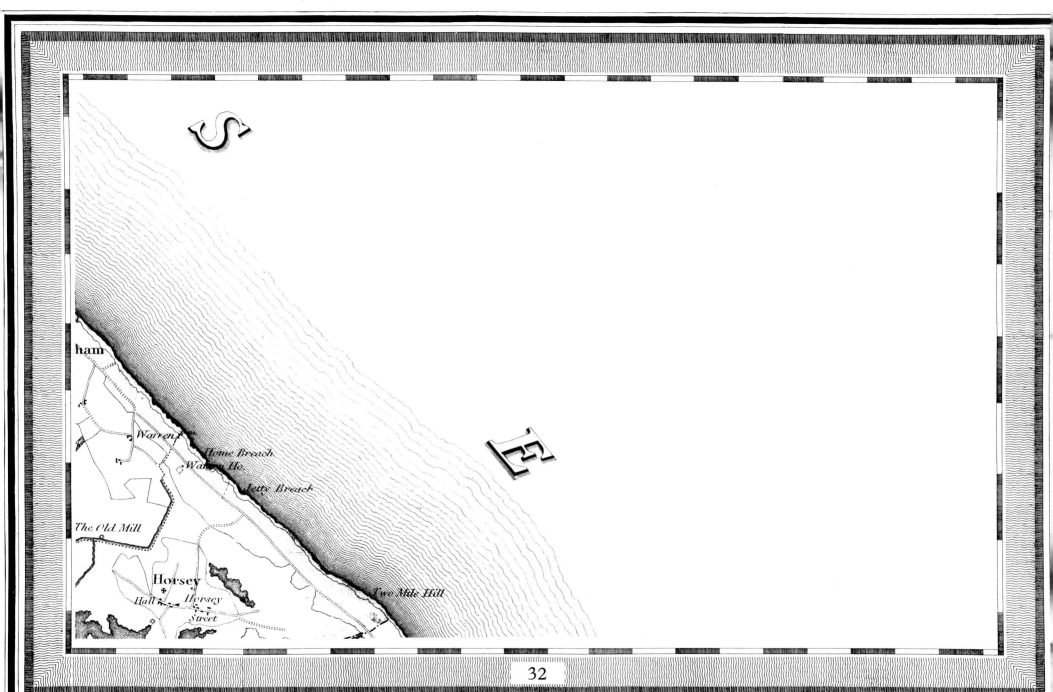

S

E

ham

Warren Fm

Home Breach

Water Ho.

Jetty Breach

The Old Mill

Horsey

Hall

Horsey
Street

Two Mile Hill

D · R · I · V · E · R

Martham Broad

Winterton Ness *Lighthouses or*
The Thoughts Lights

The Sand Width

Hitch's

S

A

East Somerton
Somerton Hall
ton ruins

Westsomerton Hall
West Somerton

Pars.^e

Preventive Lookout

Winterton
Light House

Dam Gate

Warren B.ⁿ

tham Parsonage

Bluddles

Martham Mills

Gibbet Hill

Pound Ho.

Pars^e

Martham
Hall

B.ⁿ

Hemsby Hall

Hemsby

F

E

G

G

F.^m

rick
ln

Rollesby
Tenements

Rollesby
Broad

Waters^e

F.^m

Inn₈

Rigbo's
F.m

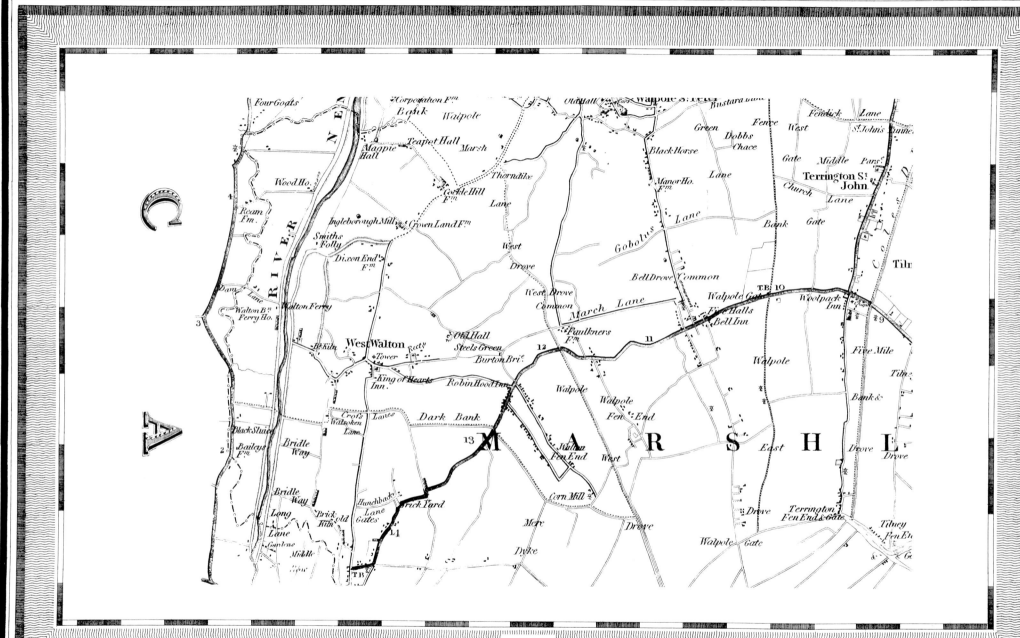

Four Goats'
NE—
Corporation F.m
Old Hall
Walpole S.t Peter
Bustard B.nk

Bank   Walpole
Marsh   Green   Dobbs   Fence   West
Teapot Hall   Black Horse   Chace   S.t John's
Magpie   Gate   Middle   Pars.
Hall   Cockle Hill   Manor Ho.   Lane   Terrington S.t
Wood Ho.   F.m   F.m   John
Thorndike   Lane   Church   Lane
Ream   4   Ingleborough Mills   Crown Land F.m   Lane   Bank   Gate
F.m   Gobolus   Lane   Tiln
Smiths   West   Lane
Folly   Drove   Bell Drove   Common   T.B. 10
Dixon End   West Drove   March Lane   Walpole Gate   Woolpack
Dam   Lane   F.m   Common   Five Halls   Inn
3   Walton B.n   Walton Ferry   Faulkners   11   Bell Inn
Ferry Ho.   Old Hall   F.m   Five Mile
B. Kiln   West Walton   Rect.y   Steels Green   12   Walpole   Tiln
Tower   Burton Bri.e   Walpole
King of Hearts   Robin Hood Inn
Inn   Walpole   Walpole   Bank &
Black Sluice   Crots   Lanes   Dark Bank   Fen End
Walsoken   Lane   13   M   A   R   S   H   East   Drove   L.
2   Baileys   Bridle   Walton   West
F.m   Way   Fen End
Corn Mill   Drove   Terrington
Bridle   Way   Drove   Fen End & Gate   Tilney
Long   Brick   Hunchback   Brick Yard   Mere   Pen End
Lane   Kiln   old   Lane   Walpole   Gate   &
Gardens   Middle   Gates   14   Dyke   Drove
T.B.

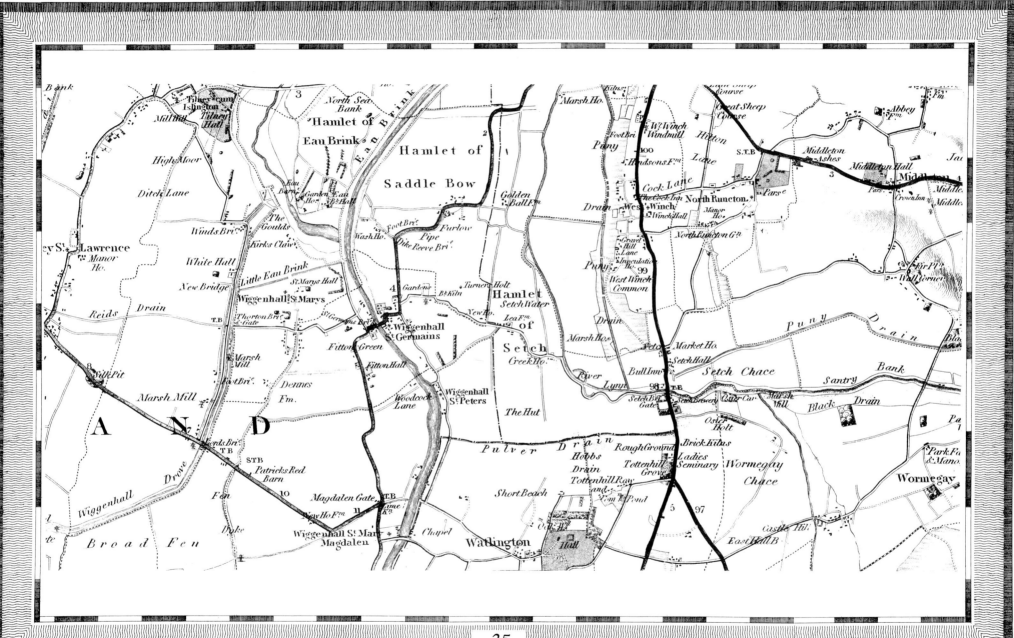

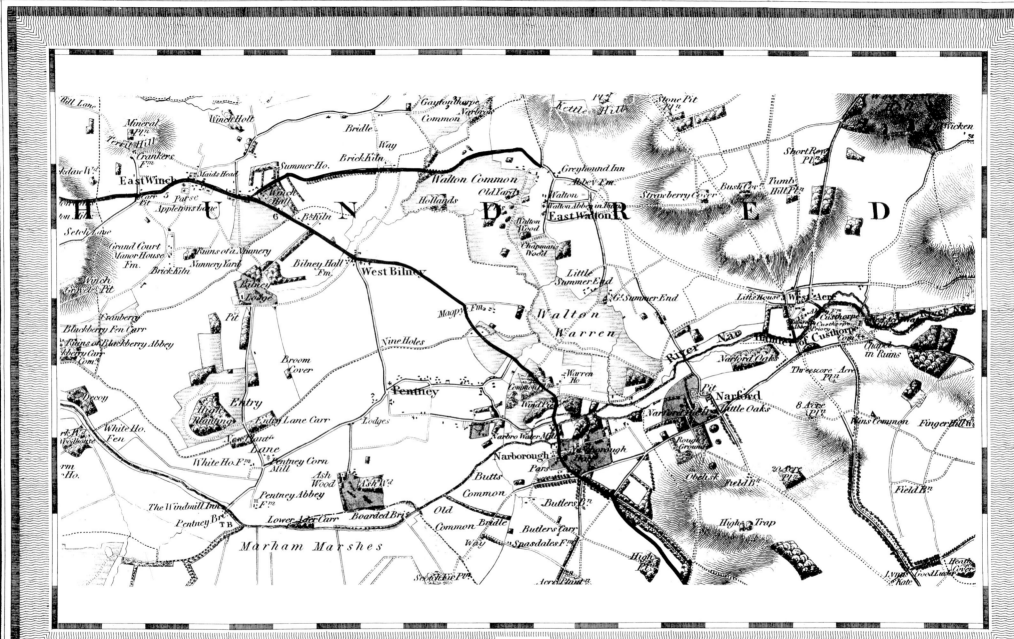

Hill Lane
Mineral Pit
Territ Hill
Crankers Fm
kdaw Wd
East Winch
Maids Head
Carr 5 Pafse
Pit
Appletons Lane
Setch Lane
6
Br Kiln
Grand Court
Manor House Fm.
Ruins of a Nunnery
Brickiln
Nunnery Yard
Winch Sifted Pit
Cranberry
Blackberry Fen Carr
Ruins of Blackberry Abbey
kberry Carr Com
Decoy
rk Wd
Wellhouse
White Ho. Fen
rm
Ho.

Windle Holt
Summer Ho.
Brickiln
Bridle
Way
Brick Kiln
Winch Hall
Bilney Hall Fm
West Bilney
Bilney Lodge
Pit
Broom Cover
Nine Holes
Entry
High Warming
Enty Lane Carr
New Plant
Lane
White Ho. Fm.
Pentney Corn Mill
Lodges
Ash Wood
Ash Wd
Pentney Abbey Fm
The Windmill Inn
Pentney Brg
T B
Lower Acre Carr
Boarded Brig
Marham Marshes

Gayton thorpe Common
Narbro
Walton Common
Old Yard
Hollands
Walton Wood
Chapmans Wood

Magpy Fm
Walton Warren
Pentney
Common
Warren Ho
Wind P
Narbro Water Mill
Narborough
Narborough Pars
Butts
Common
Old Common
Bridle Way
Butlers Carr
Spasdales Fm
High

Kettle Hill
Pit
Stone Pit

Greyhound Inn
Abbey Fm
Walton
Walton Abbey in Ruins
East Walton
Little Summer End
Gt Summer End
River Nar
Narford Oaks

Wicken
Short Row Pit
Bush Cov
Tumly Hill Pit
Strawberry Cover
Lills House
West Acre
Custhorpe
Priory
Hamlet of Custhorpe
Chapel in Ruins
Threescore Acre Pit
8 Acre Pit
Ruins Common
Finger Hill
Pit
Narford
Little Oaks
Rough Ground
Obelisk
Field Bn
30 Acre Pit
Field Bn
High Trap
Heath Cover

H U N D R E D

36

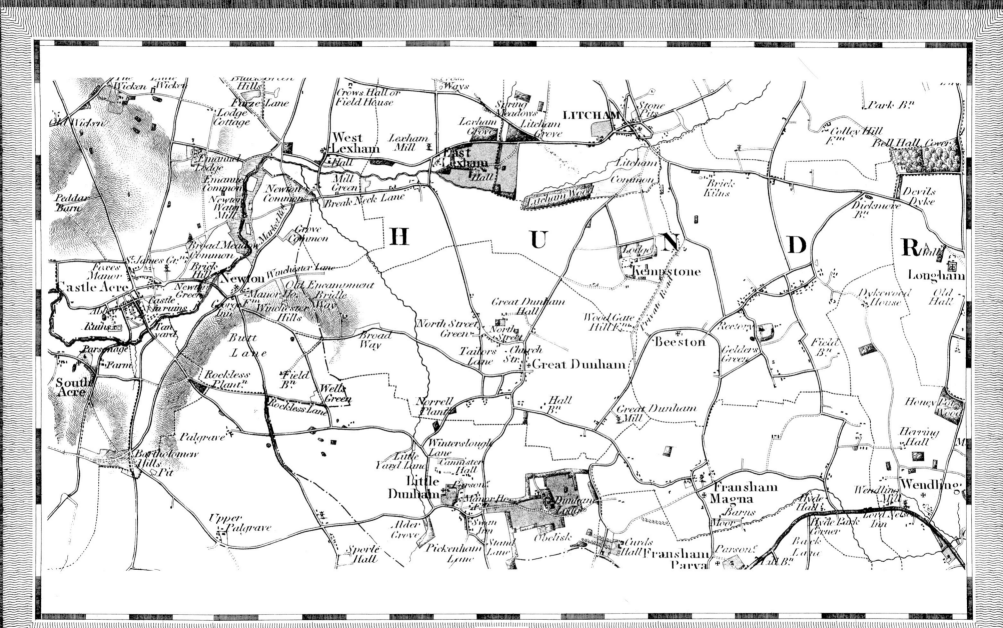

Old Wicken
The Wicken
Little Wicken
Black Green
Hills
Crows Hall or Field House
Ways

Furze Lane
Lodge Cottage

Peddar Barn

Emanuel Lodge
Emanuel Common
Newton Common
Newton Water Mill

West Lexham
East Lexham
Hall
Mill Green
Break Neck Lane
Lexham Mill

Lexham Grove
Spring Meadows
Litcham Grove

LITCHAM
Stone Pits

Park B⁰

Colley Hill
F⁰
Bell Hall Cover.

Litcham Common
Brick Kilns
Devils Dyke

Dickmore B⁰

H   U   N   D   R

Grove Common

Broad Meadow
Market Ho.
St James Gr⁰
Common
Brick Hills

Castle Acre
Foxes Manor
Newton Green
Newton
Winchester Lane
George F⁰
Castle in ruins
Manor Ho.
Bridle
Winchester Way
Hills
Old Encampment

Castle in Ruins
Abbey
Ruins
Tanyard
Inn

Parsonage
Farm

South Acre

Butt Lane
Broad Way

Rockless Plant⁰
Field B⁰
Wells Green
Rockless Lane

Kempstone
Lodge

Longham

Dykewood House
Old Hall

Great Dunham Hall
North Street Green
North Street
Church Str.
Tailors Lane
Great Dunham

Wood Gate Hill F⁰
Private Road
Beeston
Rectory
Gelders Green

Field B⁰

Norrell Plant⁰
Hall B⁰
Great Dunham Mill
Great Dunham

Honey Pot Wood

Herring Hall

Palgrave
Winterslough Lane
Little Yard Lane
Tanmster Hall

Bartholomew Hills
Pit
Little Dunham
Manor Ho.
Parsons
Dunham Lodge

Fransham Magna
Barns
Moor
Wendling Mill
Wendling

Upper Palgrave
Alder Grove
Swan Inn
Stand Lane
Obelisk
Curds Hall
Fransham Parva
Parson⁰
Hyde Hall
Hyde Park Corner
Back Lane
Lord Nelson Inn
Mill B⁰

Sporle Hall
Pickenham Lane

37

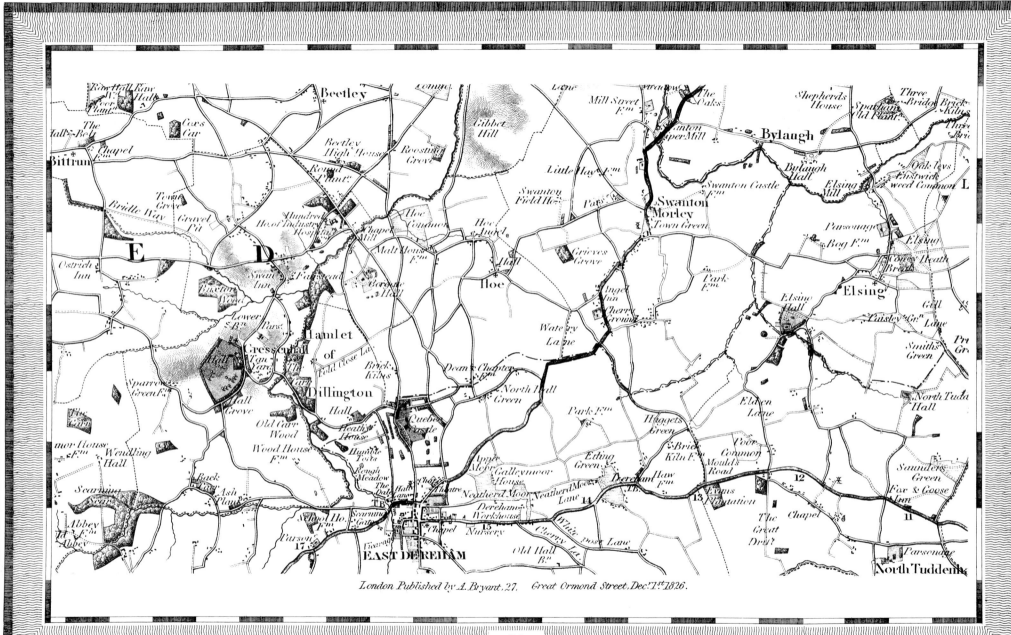

London Published by A. Bryant, 27. Great Ormond Street, Dec.r 1.st 1826.

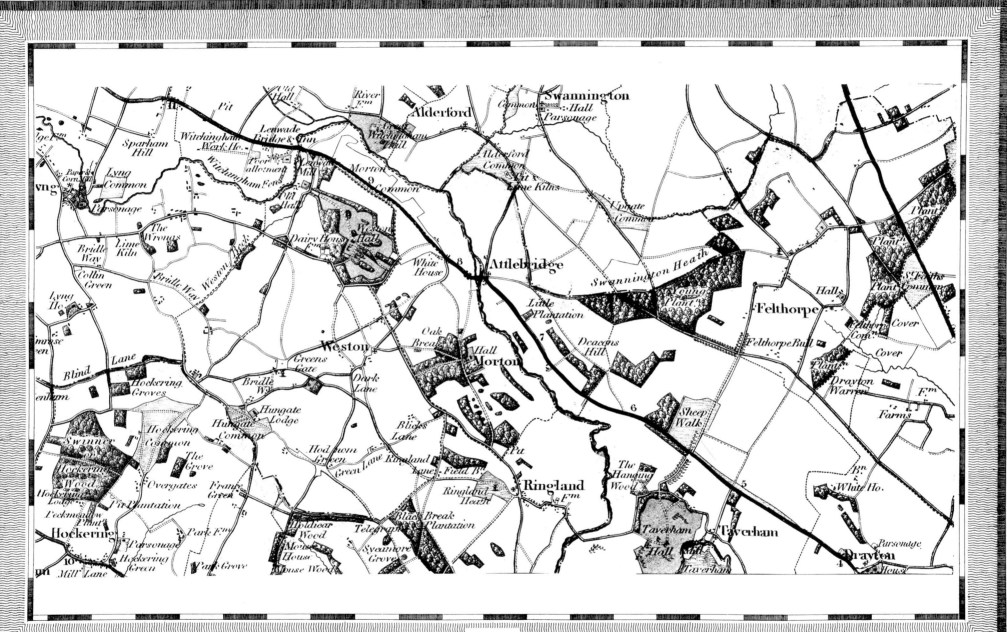

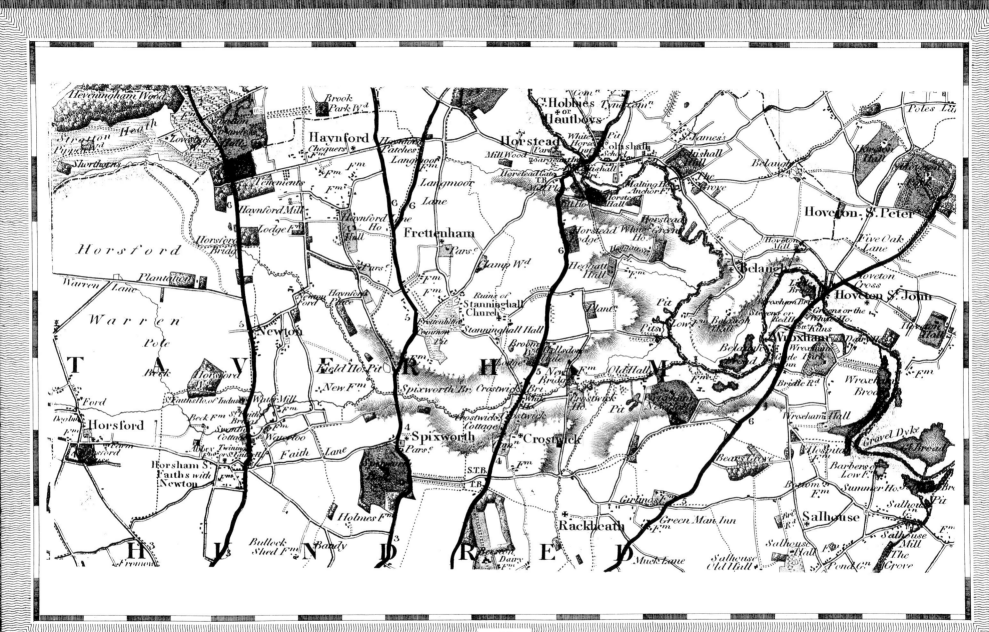

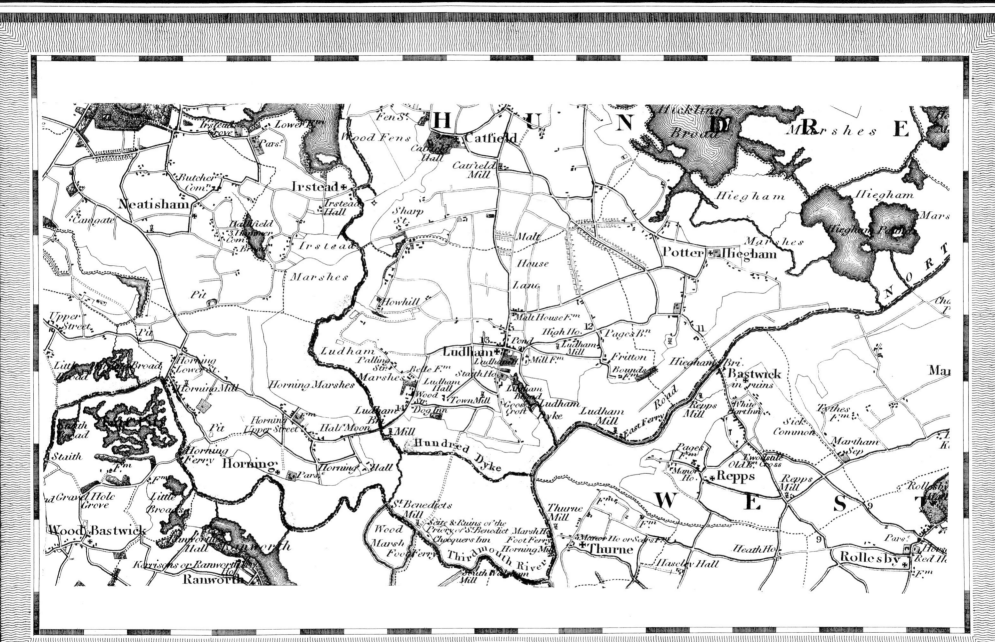

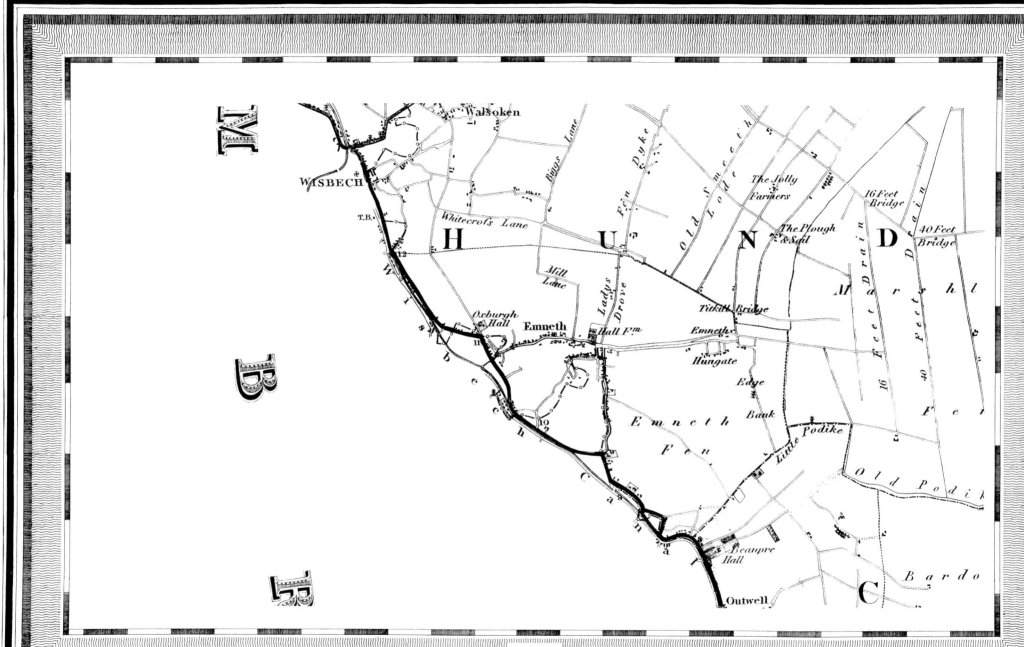

M

Walsoken

WISBECH

H U N D

Biggs Lane

Fen Dyke

Old Smeeth

The Jolly Farmers

16 Feet Bridge

Whitecrofs Lane

The Plough & Sail

40 Feet Bridge

T.B.

Mill Lane

Ladys Drove

N

Feet Drain

M a r s h l

B

Oxburgh Hall

Emneth

Hall Fm

Tikill Bridge

Emneth

16 Feet Drain

40 Feet Drain

Hungate

Edge

Bank

Emneth Fen

Little Podike

Old Podik

F e n

Beaupre Hall

B a r d o

R

Outwell

C

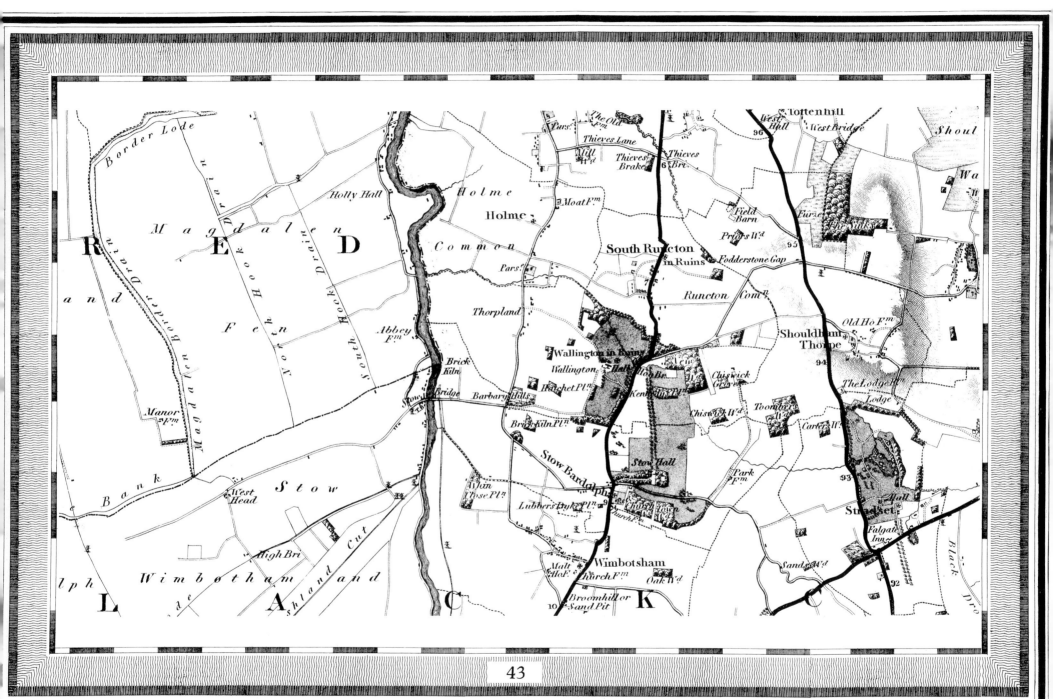

43

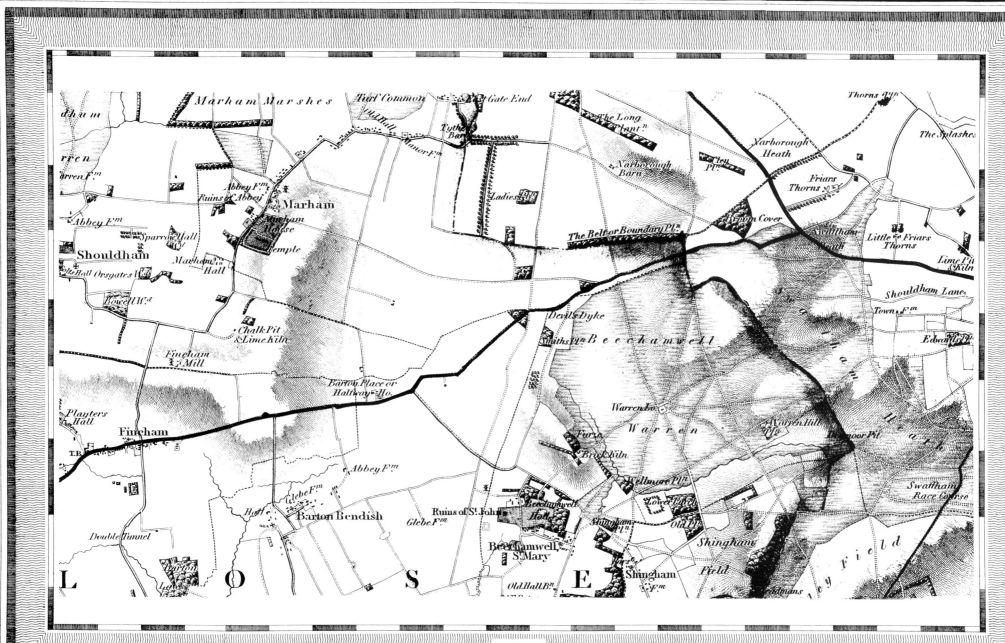

Marham Marshes

Turf Common

Gate End

The Long Plant'n

Thorns Plt'n

The Splashes

dham

Old Hall

Manor Fm

Tythe Barn

Narborough Barn

Narborough Heath

rren

Ladies

Crst Plt

Friars Thorns

Abbey Fm

Ruins of Abbey

Marham

Devon Cover

Swaffham

Abbey Fm

Sparrow Hall

Marham House

Little Friars Thorns

Shouldham

Temple

The Belt or Boundary Plt'n

Lime Pit & Kiln

Marham Hall

Old Hall Orsgates

Devils Dyke

Shouldham Lane

Bowell Wd

Town Fm

Chalk Pit & Lime Kiln

Smiths Plt'n

Beechamwell

Edward Fm

Fincham Mill

Playters Hall

Barton Place or Halfway Ho.

Warren Lo

Warren

Warren Hill

Bagmoor Pit

Fincham

Furze

Brick Kiln

Swaffham Race Course

T.B.

Abbey Fm

Wellmore Pit

Glebe Fm

Hall

Barton Bendish

Glebe Fm

Ruins of St John

Beechamwell Hall

Lower Fen

Old Pit

Double Tunnel

Barton

Beechamwell St Mary

Shingham Plt'n

Shingham

Field

Shingham Fm

L   O   S   E

Old Hall Bn

dmans

44

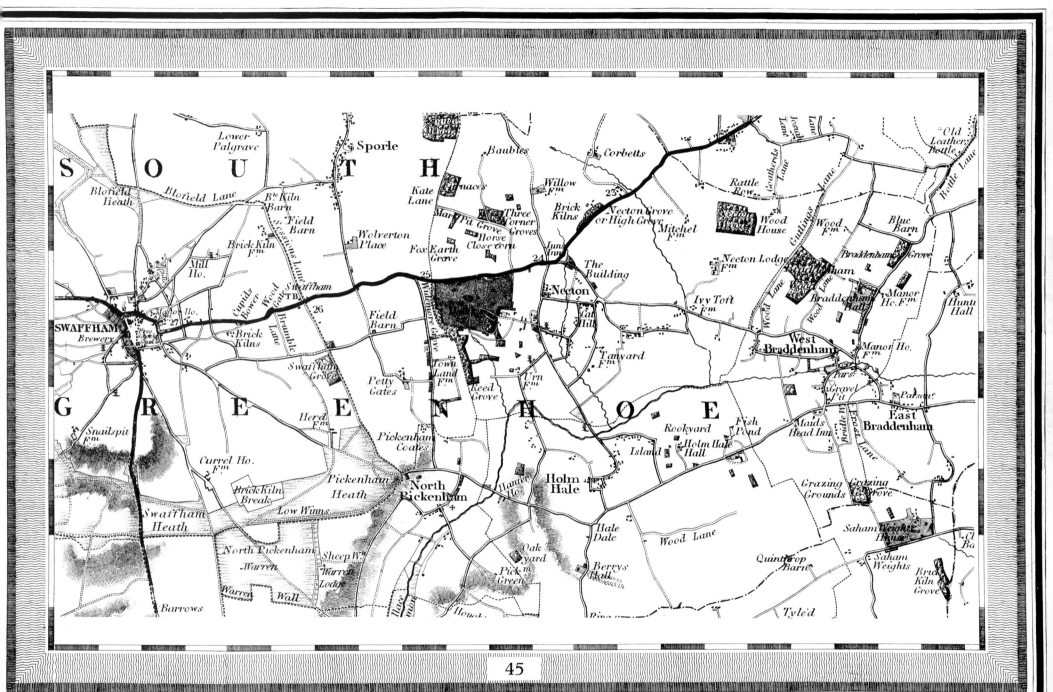

S O U T H

Lower
Palgrave

Sporle

Baubles

Corbetts

Blofield
Heath

Blofield Lane

B^k Kiln
Barn

Furnaces

Kate
Lane

Willow
F^m

Rattle
Row

Old
Leather
Bottle

Field
Barn

Sessions Lane

Wolverton
Place

Marsh

Three
Corner
Groves

Brick
Kilns

Necton Grove
or High Grove

Mitchel
F^m

Necton
Wood
House

Wood
F^m

Blue
Barn

Brick Kiln
F^m

Mill
Ho.

Pit Grove
Close corn

Horse

Necton Lodge
F^m

Braddenham Grove

Fox Earth
Grove

Inns
Inn

24

The
Building

Cupids
Bower

Wood
Gates

Swaffham

25

Wildmore Grove

Necton

Ivy Toft

Braddenham
Hall

Manor
Ho. F^m

Huntu
Hall

T B

26

Brumble Lane

Field
Barn

Cat
Hill

Wood Lane

SWAFFHAM
Brewery

27

Malton Ho.

Three
Goat

Brick
Kilns

Town
Land
F^m

Tanyard

West
Braddenham

Manor Ho.
F^m

Manor Ho.

G R E E N

Swaffham
Grove

Herd
F^m

Petty
Gates

Reed
Grove

Urn
F^m

H O E

Rookyard

Fish
Pond

Maids
Head Inn

Pars

Gravel
Pit

Parso

East
Braddenham

Snailspit
F^m

Pickenham
Coates

Island

Holm Hale
Hall

Grazing
Grounds

Grazing
Grove

Currel Ho.
F^m

Pickenham
Heath

North
Pickenham

Hanter
Ho.

Holm
Hale

Saham Weights
House

Cl
Ba

Brick Kiln
Break

Swaffham
Heath

Low Winns

Hale
Dale

Wood Lane

Quinthrop
Barn

Saham
Weights

Brick
Kiln
Grove

North Pickenham
Warren

Sheep W.

Oak
yard

Berrys
Hall

Warren
Lodge

Pick^m
Green

Warren Wall

Barrows

House

Ring

Tyle'd

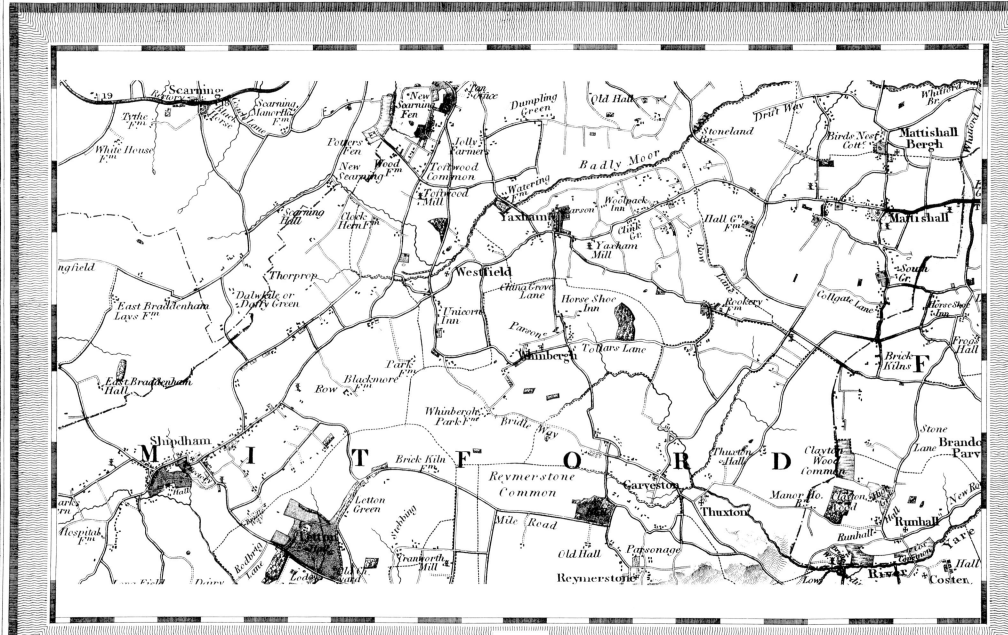

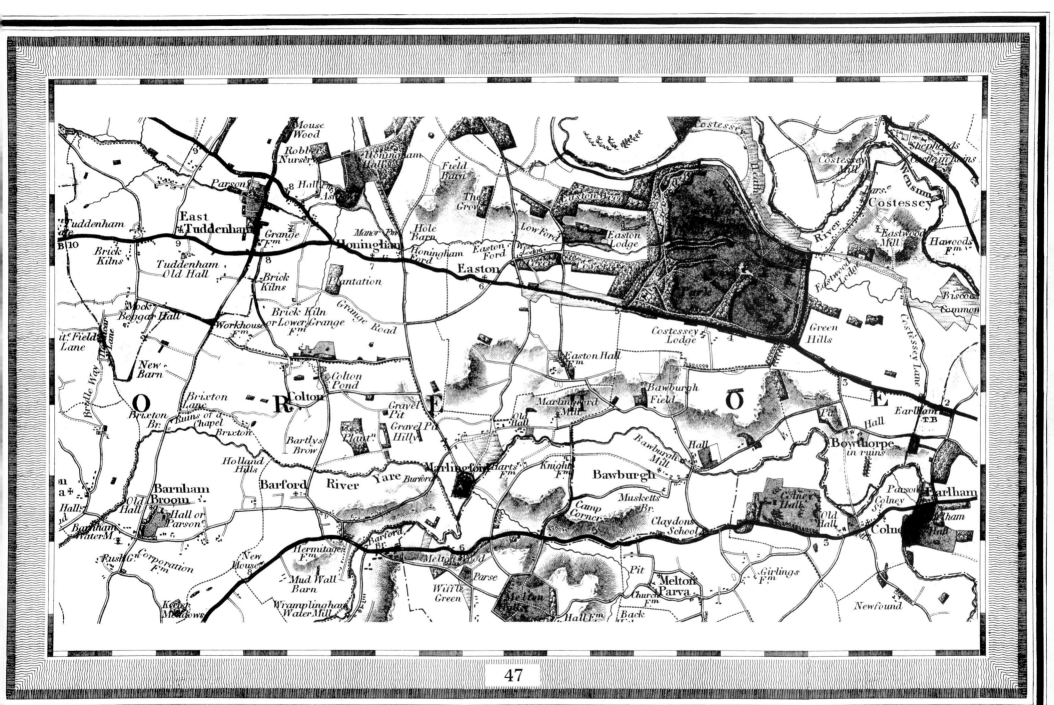

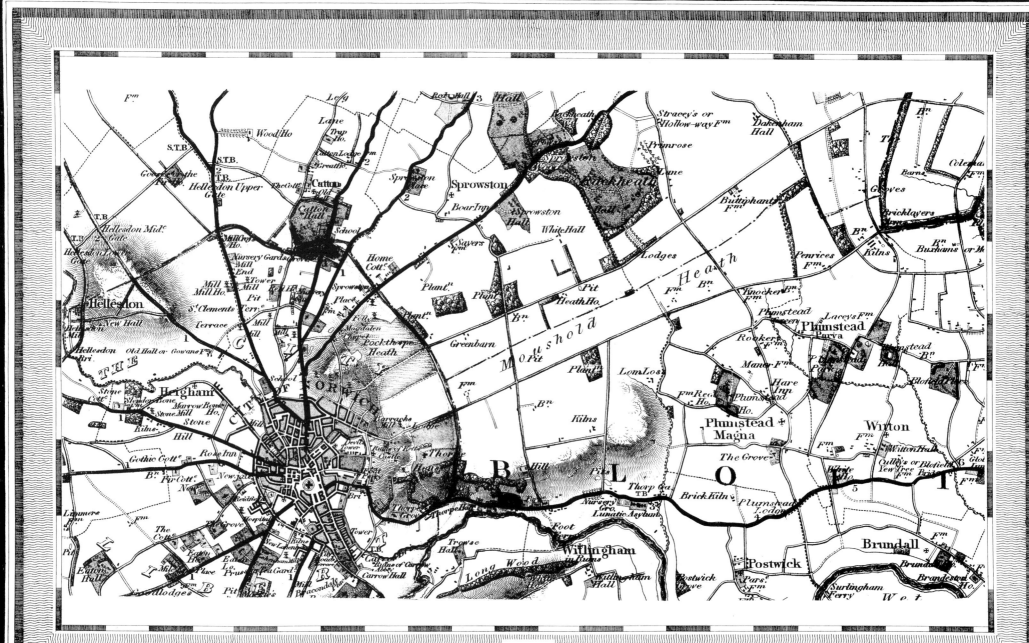

48

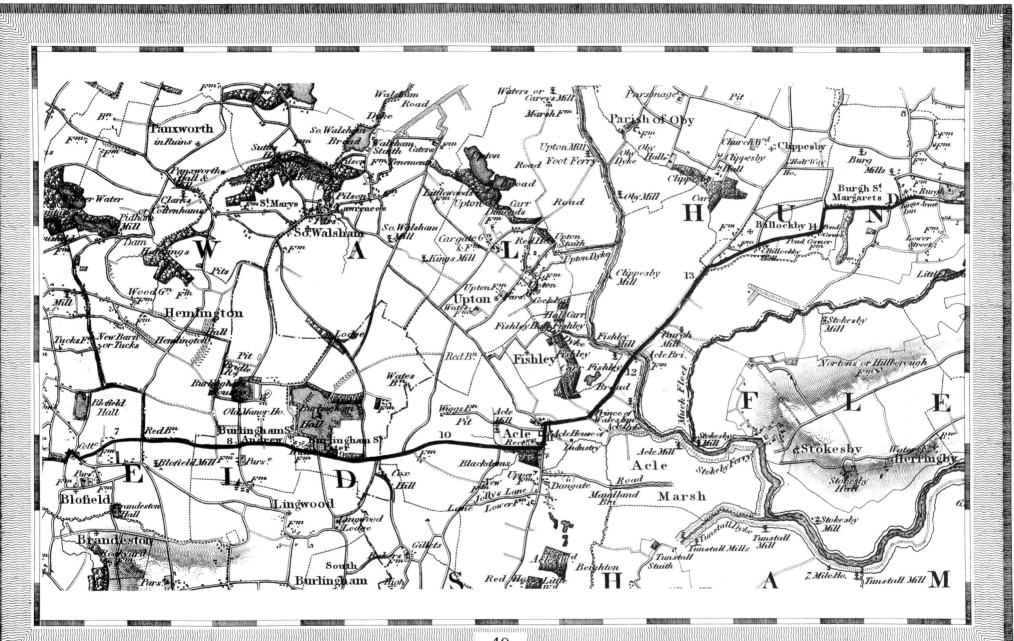

Panxworth in Ruins

Panxworth Hall &

Clarks or Cottenhams

Water Plantation

Pidham Mill

Dam

Hastings

Wood Gn

Hemington

Hemington Hall

New Barn or Tucks

Hemingtoll

Tucks Fm

Pits

Bridle Rd.

Burlingham House

Old Manor Ho.

Burlingham Hall

Blofield Hall

Blofield

Brandeston Hall

Brandeston

Rookyard

Pars.

Blofield Mill

Burlingham St. Andrew

Burlingham St. Peter

Lingwood

Lingwood Lodge

Cox Hill

Bakers Fm

Gillets

South Burlingham

So. Walsham Broad

Suttons Hall

St. Marys

So. Walsham

St. Lawrences

So. Walsham Mill

Kings Mill

Walsham Road

Walsham Staith

Caters

Alson

Tenements

Littlewoods

Upton Broad

Cargate Gn & Fm

Upton

Upton Fm

Red Ho.

Waters Fm

Fishley Hall

Fishley

Red Bn

Fishley Broad

Wates Bn

Wiggs Fm

Pit

Acle Hall

Acle

Acle House or Acle Dyke

Blackdams

New Jolly's Lane

Lower Fm

Dangate

Maudland Bri.

Acle Wd

Little Wd

Red Ho.

Beighton

Waters or Careys Mill

Marsh Fm

Upton Mill

Foot Ferry

Oby Dyke

Oby Hall

Oby Mill

Carr Road

Chippesby Mill

Fishley Mill

Burgh Mill

Acle Bri.

Muck Fleet

Prince of Wales Inn

Acle Dyke

Acle Mill

Acle Road

Marsh

Upton Staith

Cock Fm

Hall Carr

Carr Fishley

Broad

Parish of Oby

Parsonage

Church Yard

Chippesby Hall

Chippesby

Billockby 14

Billockby Hall

Pit

Half Way

Burg Mills

Burgh St. Margarets

Pond Corner

Lower Street

Stokesby Mill

Nortons or Hillborough Fm

Stokesby Mill

Stokesby

Stokesby Ferry

Stokesby Hall

Herringby

Tunstall Dyke

Tunstall Mill

Tunstall Staith

Tunstall Mills

7 Mile Ho.

Tunstall Mill

W A L S H A M

F L E G

H U N D

B L O F I E L D H U N D

49

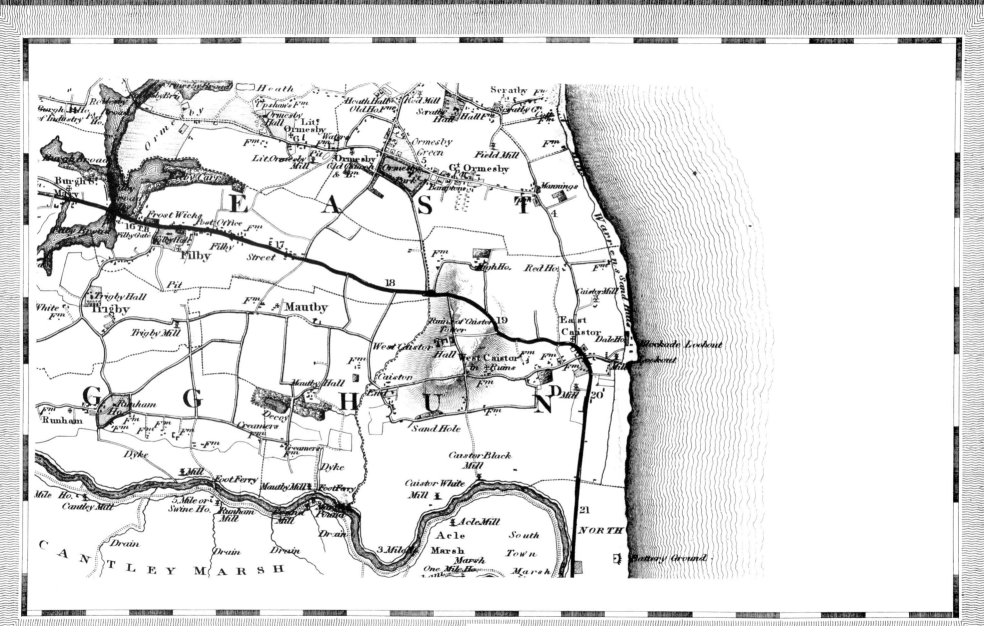

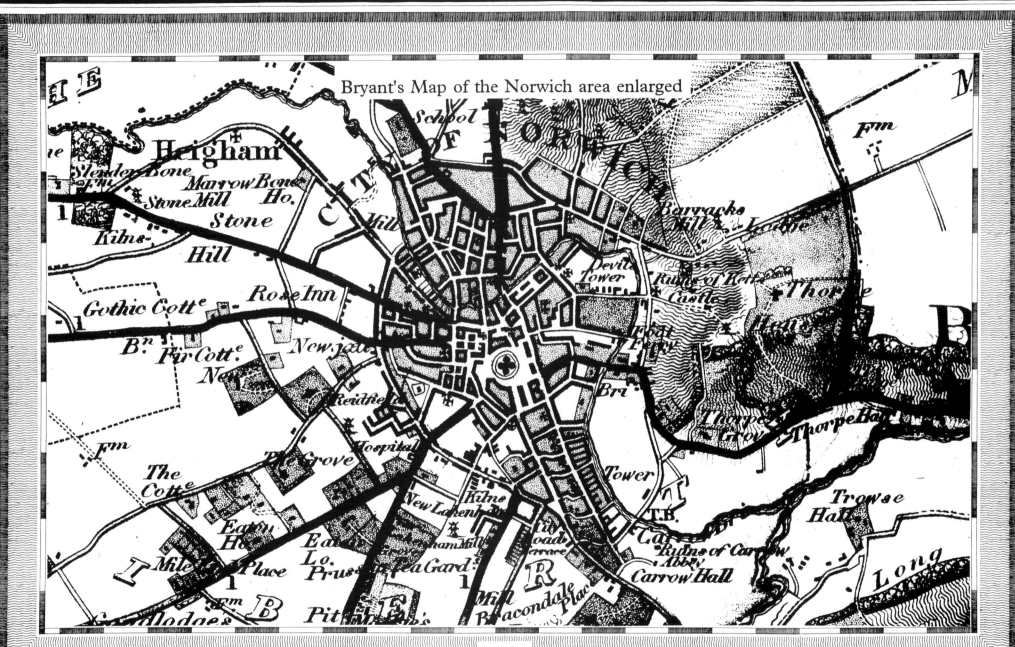

Bryant's Map of the Norwich area enlarged

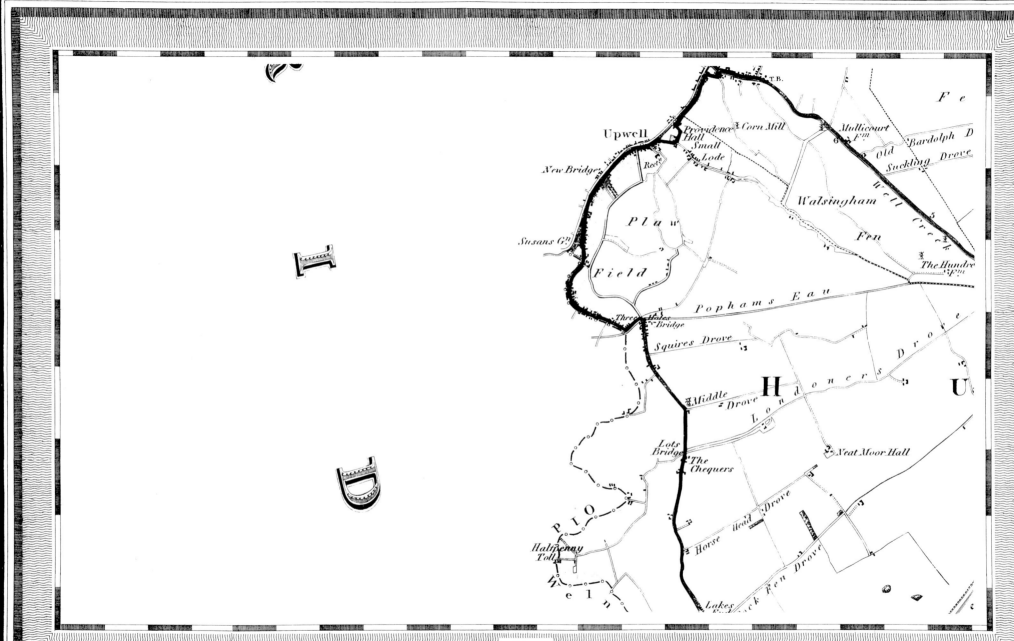

Upwell

New Bridge

Providence Hall

Small Lode

Rect²

Corn Mill

Mullicourt Fm

Bardolph D

Old Suckling Drove

Well Creek

Walsingham Fen

Plaw

Field

Susans Gⁿ

The Hundreᵈ Fm

Pophams Eau

Three Holes Bridge

Squires Drove

Londoners Drove

Middle Drove

Lots Bridge

The Chequers

Neat Moor Hall

Head Drove

Halfpenny Toll

Horse Head Drove

Beck Fen Drove

Welney

Lakes

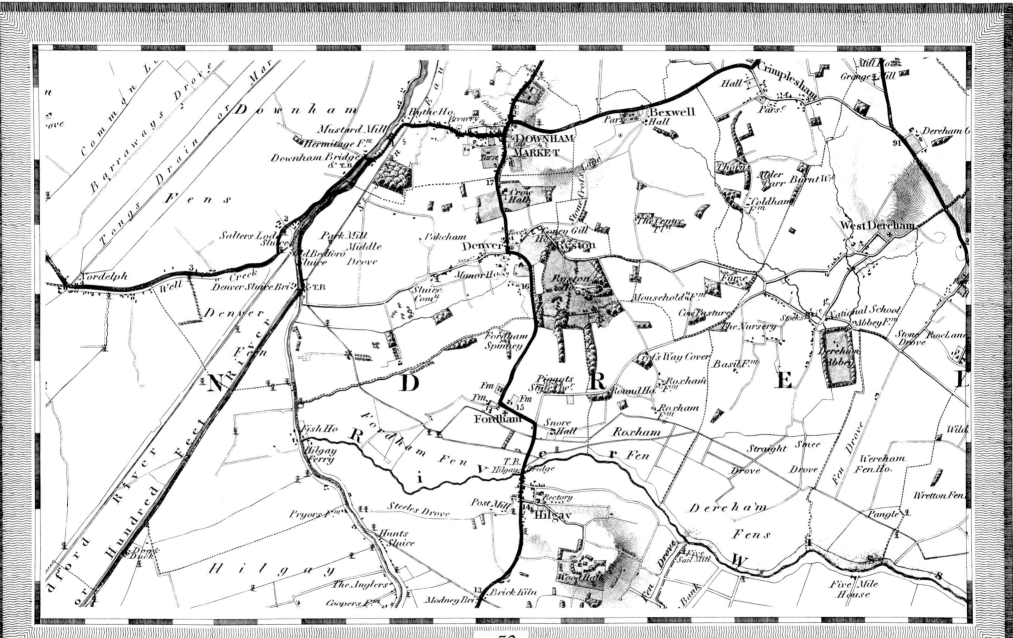

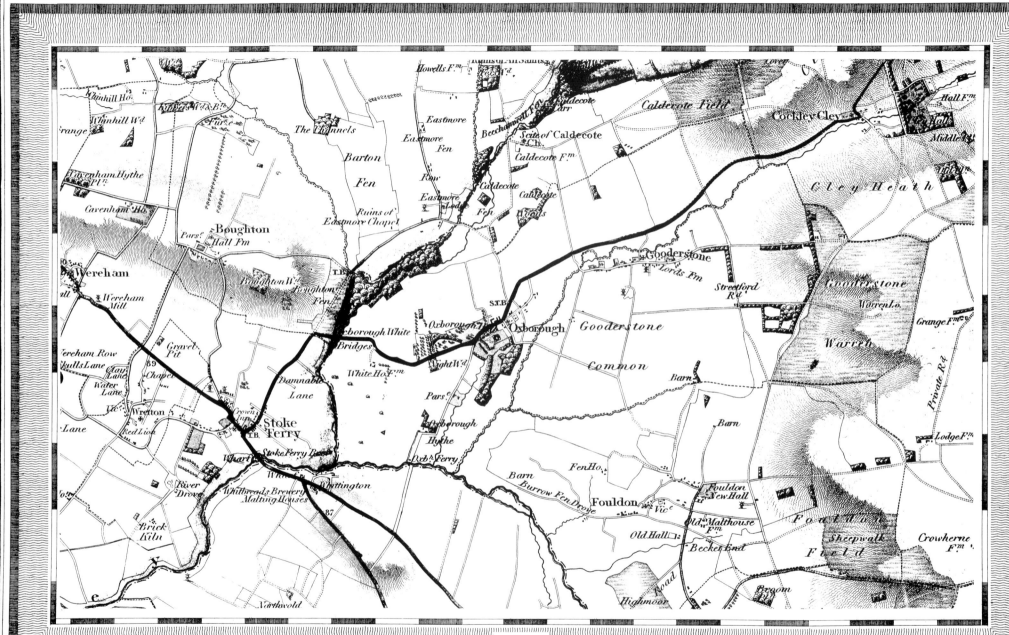

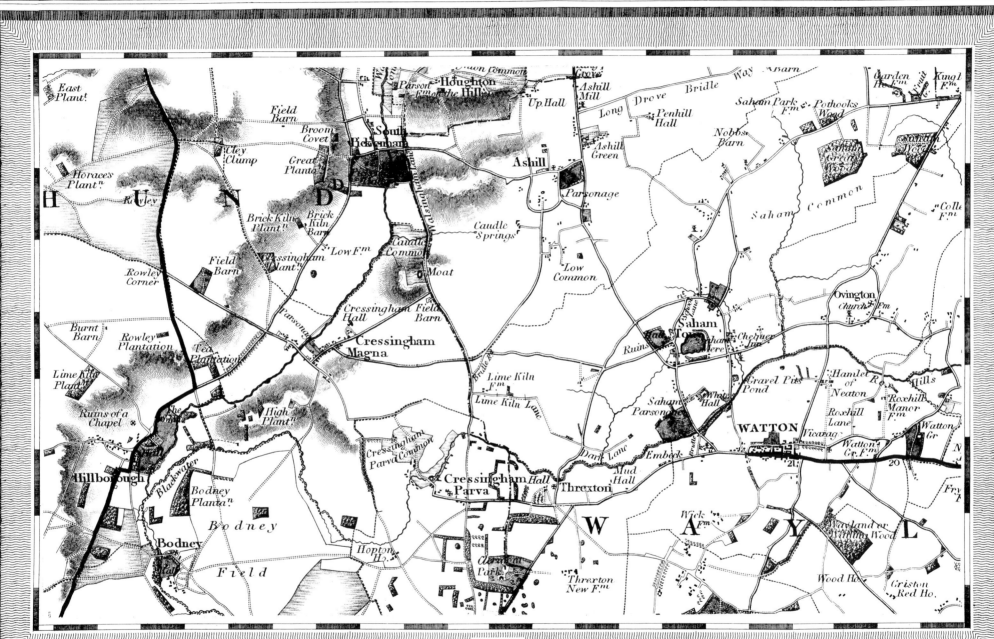

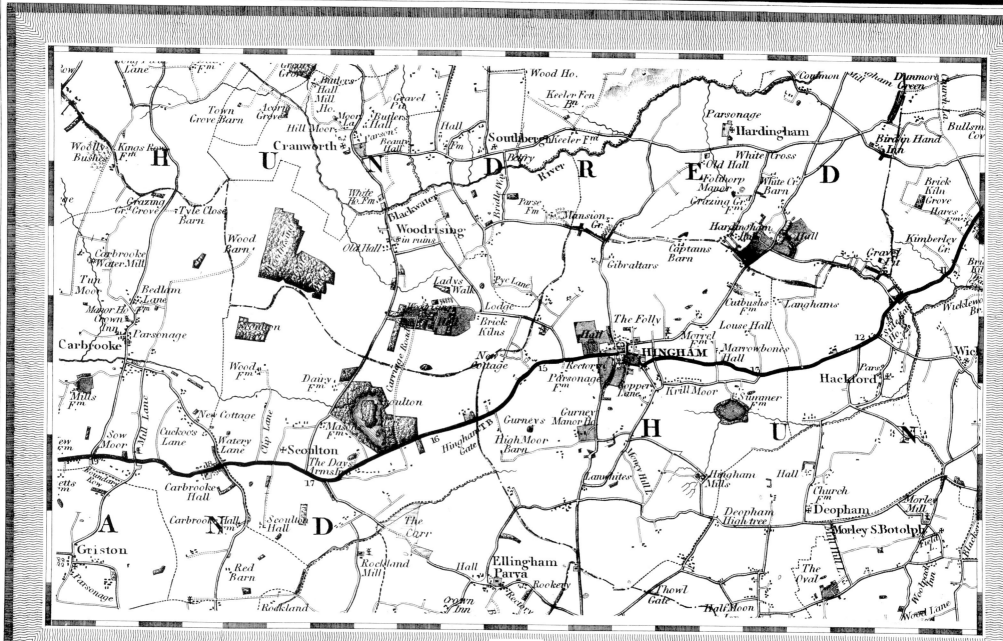

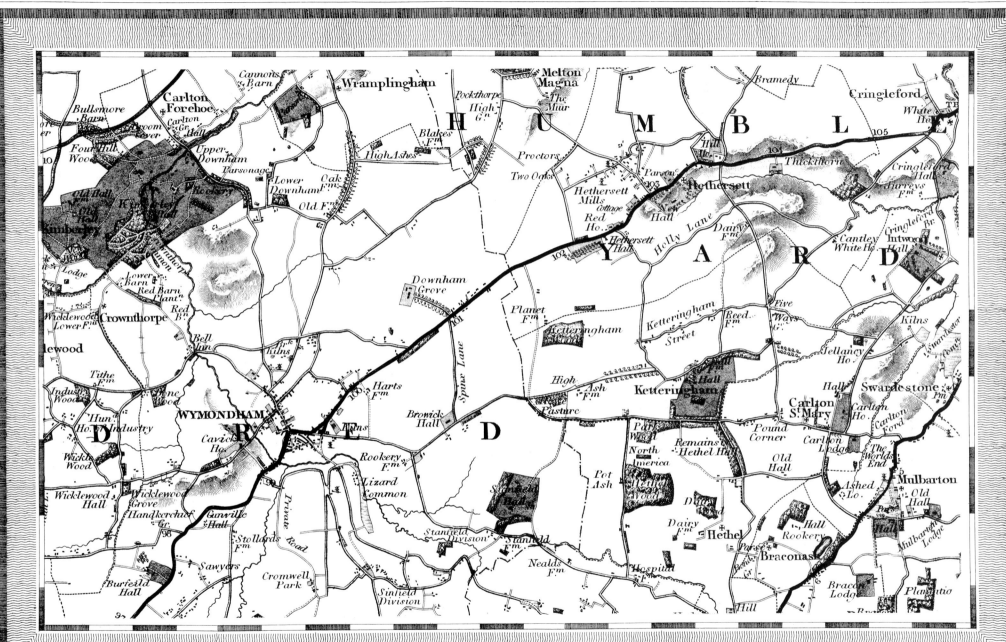

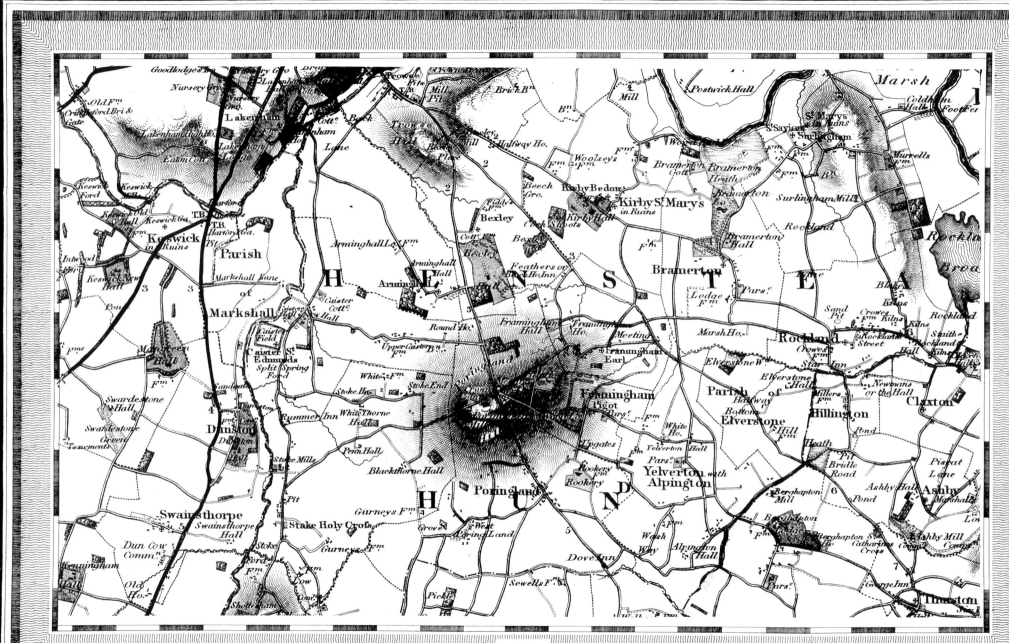

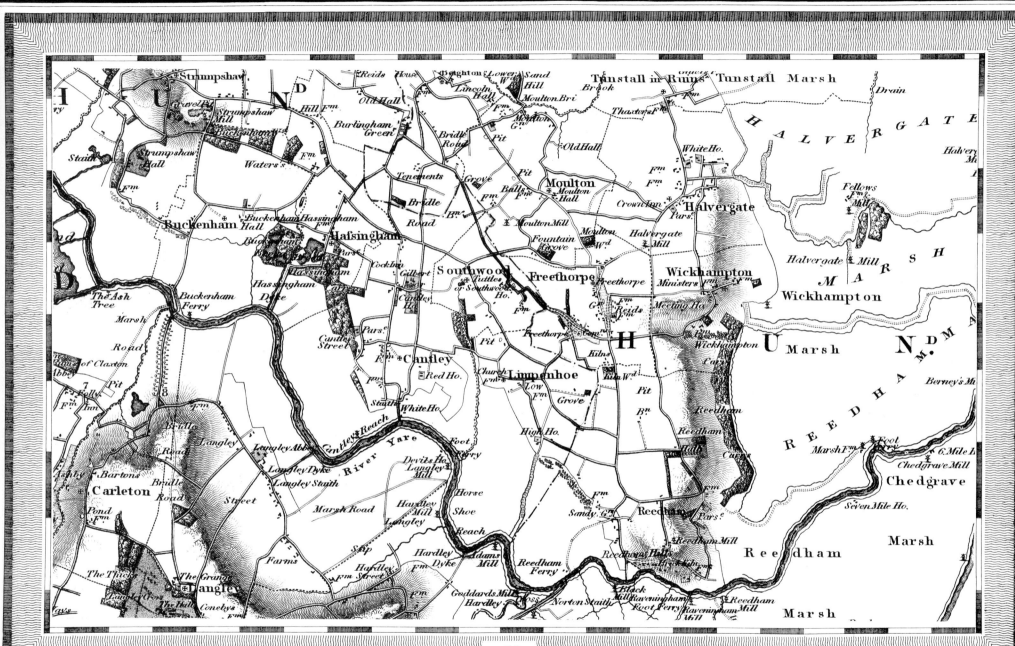

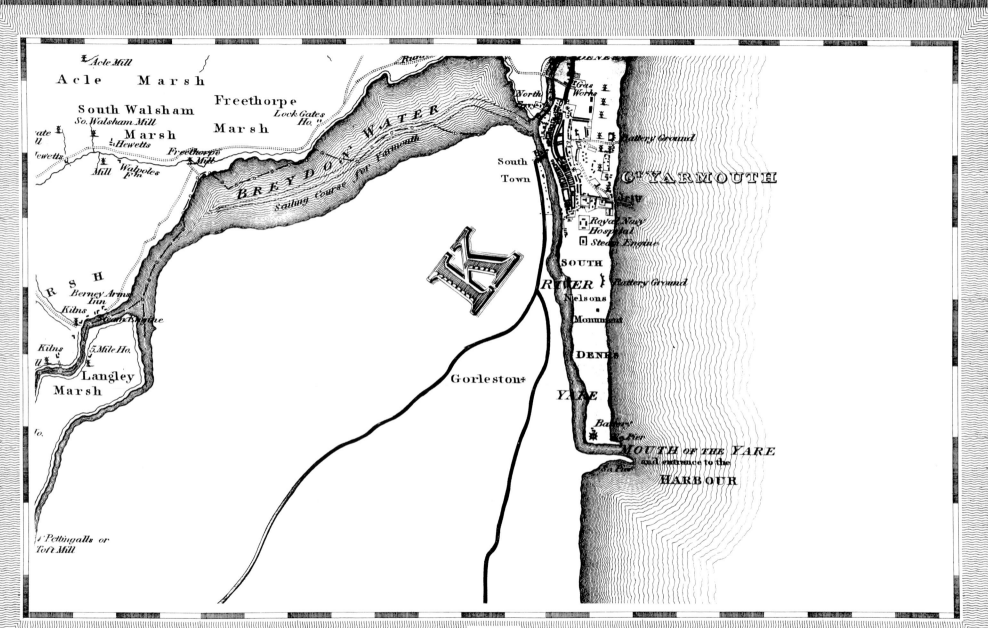

Acle Mill

Acle Marsh

South Walsham
Marsh

So. Walsham Mill

Hewetts

Freethorpe
Marsh

Lock Gates
Ho."

Freethorpe
Mill

Walpoles
F'm

Mill

RSH

Berney Arms
Inn

Kilns

Steam Engine

Kilns

5.Mile Ho.

Langley
Marsh

Pettingalls or
Toft Mill

BREYDON WATER

Sailing Course for Yarmouth

North

Gas
Works

G? YARMOUTH

Battery Ground

South
Town

Royal Navy
Hospital

Steam Engine

SOUTH

RIVER

Battery Ground

Nelsons

Monument

DENES

YARE

Gorleston*

Battery

Ho. Pier

MOUTH of the YARE
and entrance to the

HARBOUR

Sea Pier

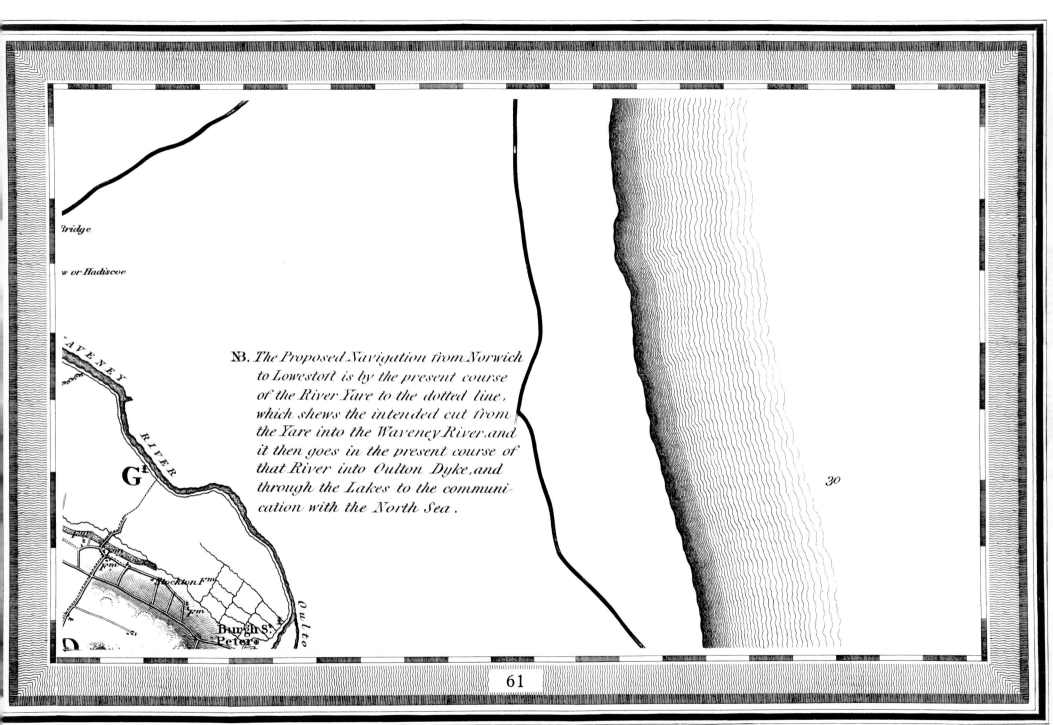

Bridge

s or Hadiscoe

WAVENEY

RIVER

G.

NB. *The Proposed Navigation from Norwich*
to Lowestoft is by the present course
of the River Yare to the dotted line,
which shews the intended cut from
the Yare into the Waveney River, and
it then goes in the present course of
that River into Oulton Dyke, and
through the Lakes to the communi-
cation with the North Sea.

Stockton F^m

F^m

Burgh S.t
Peters

Oulto

D

30

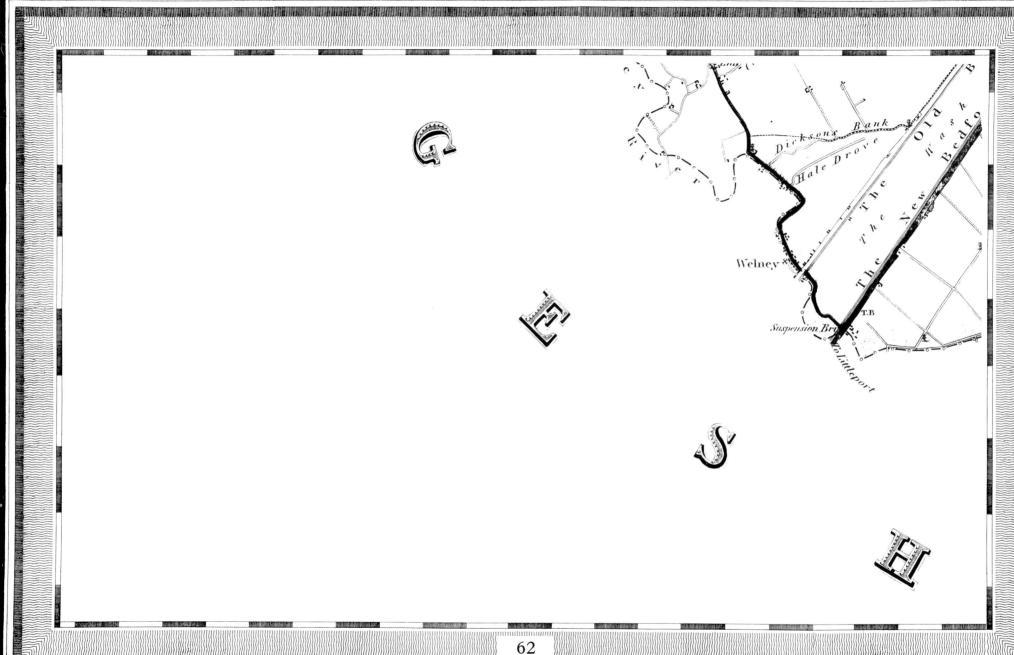

River

Dickson's Bank

Hale Drove

The Old Wash

The New Bedfo B

Welney

The

T.B

Suspension Br

To Littleport

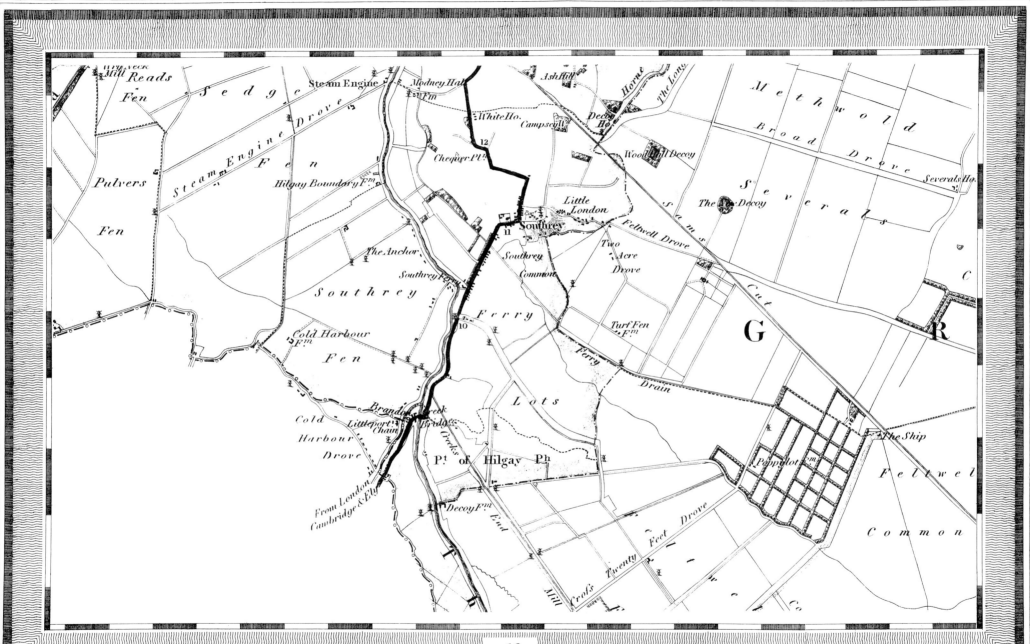

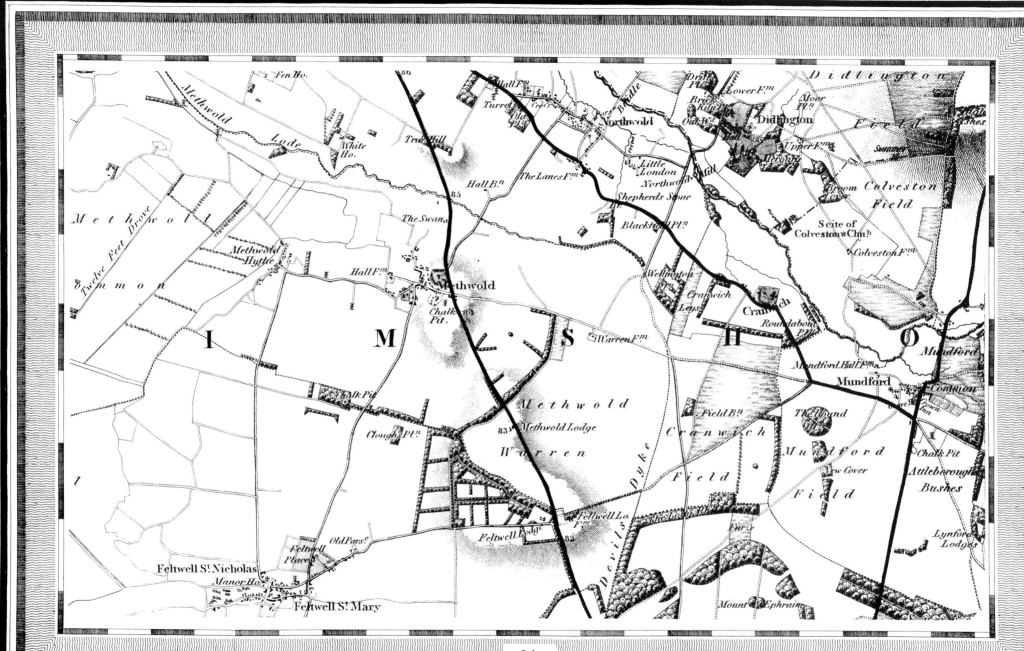

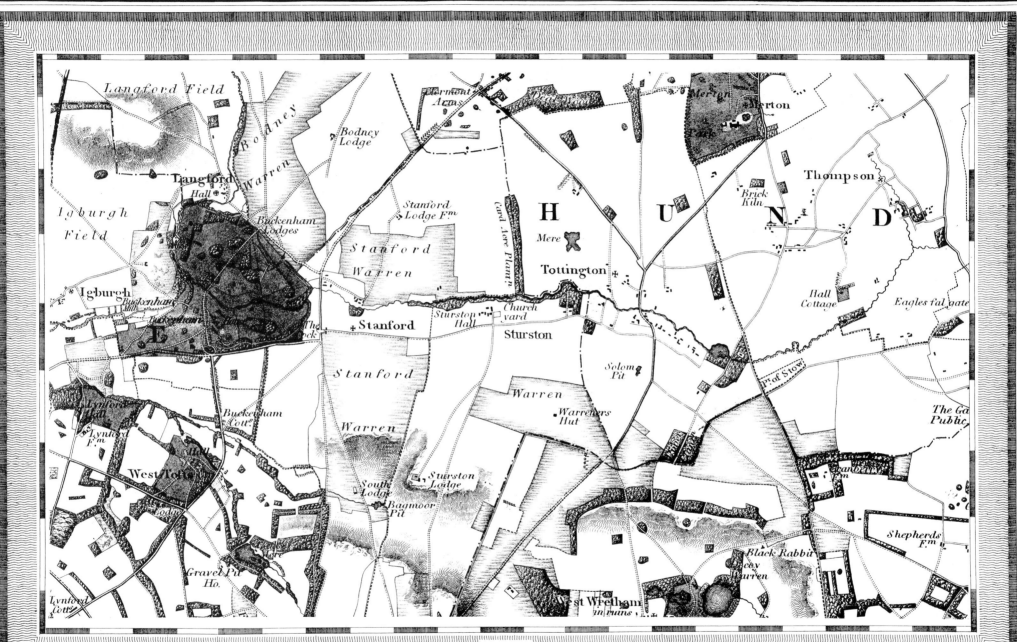

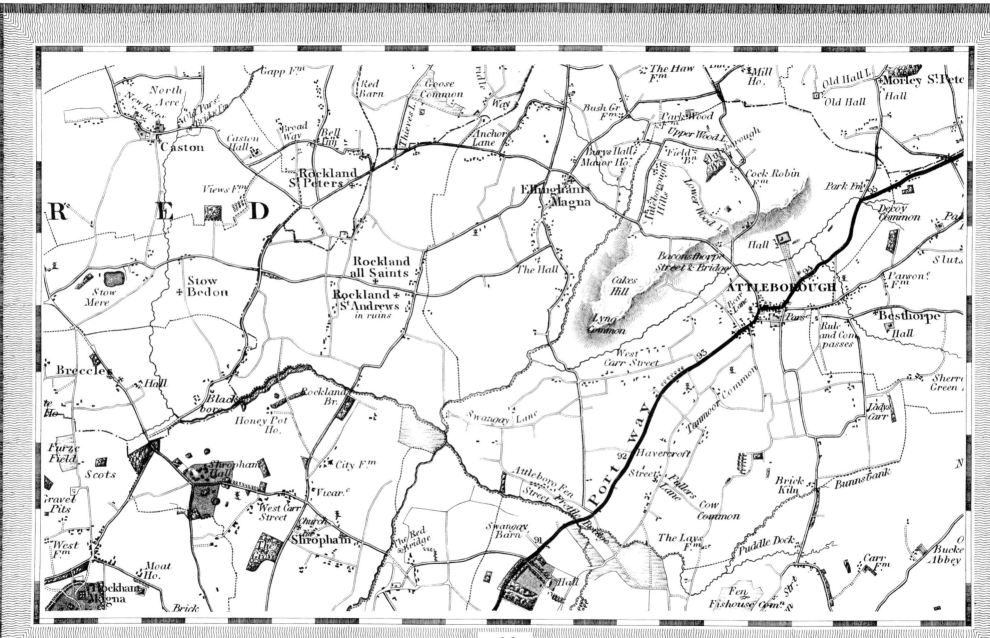

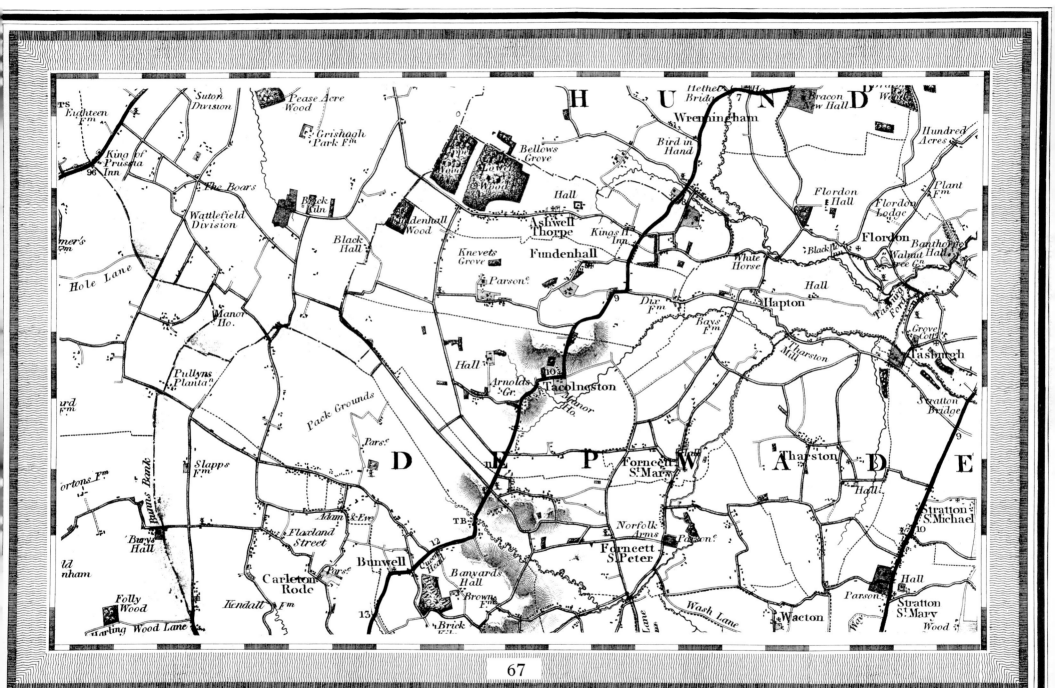

Suton
Division

Pease Acre
Wood

Eighteen
Fm

Grishagh
Park Fm

HUN
Hethel...Ho
Bridge 7

ND

Bracon
New Hall

Wremingham

Hundred
Acres

King of
Prussia
Inn
96

The Boars

Black
Kiln

Pill
Wood

Low
Wood

Bellows
Grove

Bird in
Hand

Flordon
Hall

Flordon
Lodge

Plant
Fm

Wattlefield
Division

Fundenhall
Wood

Hall

Ashwell
Thorpe

Flordon

mer's
Fm

Black
Hall

Knevets
Grove

Kings H
Inn

Fundenhall

Black Ho

Banthorpe
Walnut Hall
Tree Gr.

Hole Lane

Parson.e

White
Horse

Hall

Tasburg
Ford

Manor
Ho.

Dix
Fm

9

Hapton

Grove
Cott.

Bays
Fm

Tasburgh

Pullyns
Plantan

Hall

Tharston
Mill

Pack Grounds

Arnolds
Gr.

10
Tacolnston

Stratton
Bridge

Manor
Ho.

9

D

E

P

W

A

D

E

Pars.e

Forncett
St Mary

Tharston

Slapps
Fm

ortons Fm

Butts Bank

Adam & Eve

Hall

Stratton
St Michael

Burys
Hall

Flaxland
Street

TB

Norfolk
Arms

Parson.e

10

Folly
Wood

Parse

Bunwell

Quee Head

12

Forncett
St Peter

Wacton

Hall

nham

Carleton
Rode

Banyards
Hall

Wash Lane

Parson.

Stratton
St Mary

Kendall
Fm

Browns
Fm

Wood

Harling Wood Lane

13

Brick
Kiln

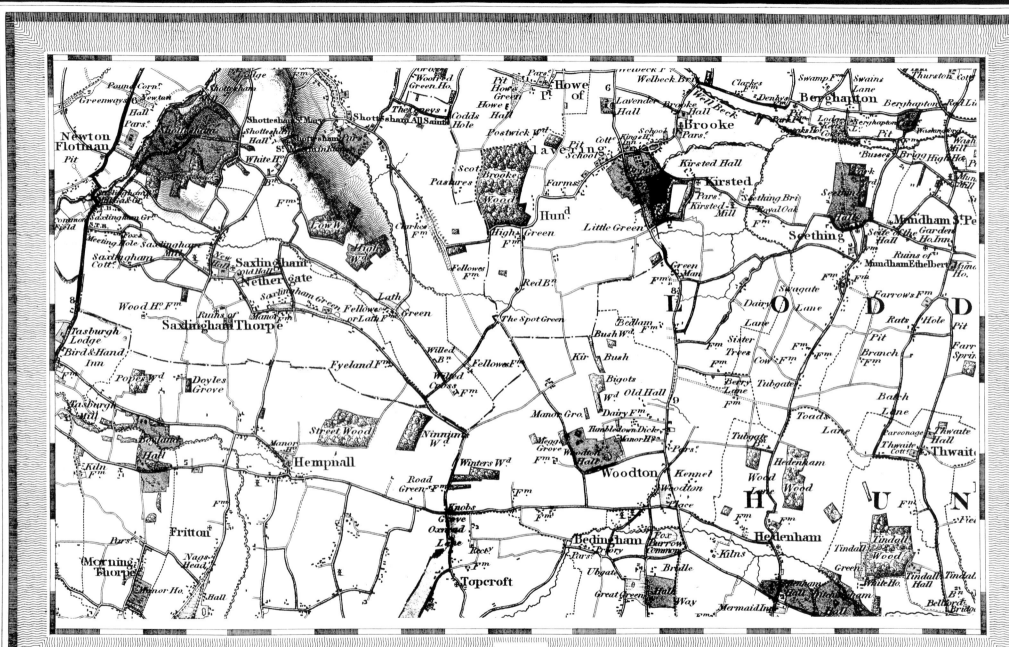

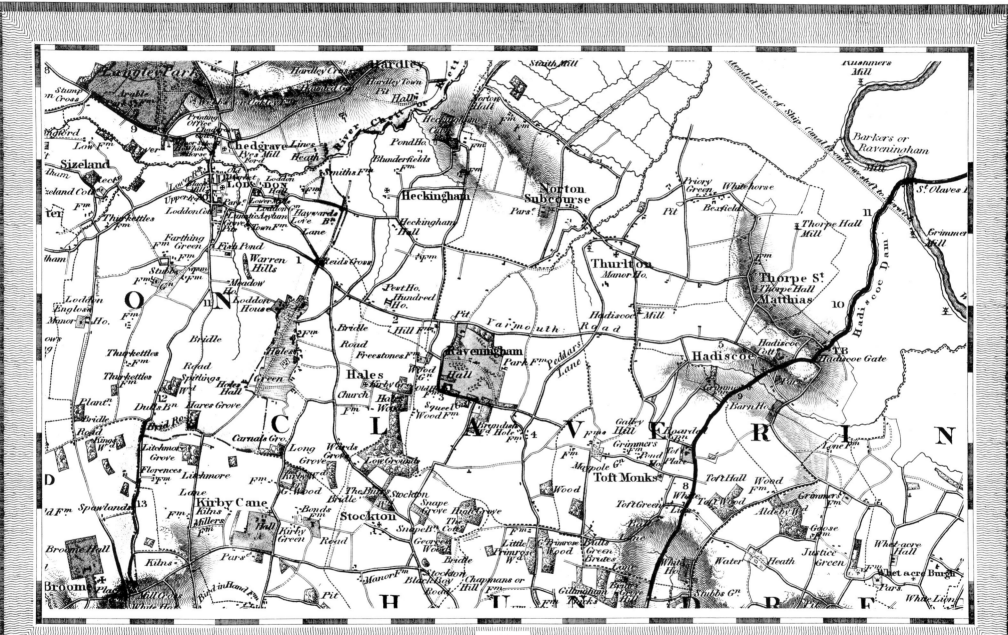

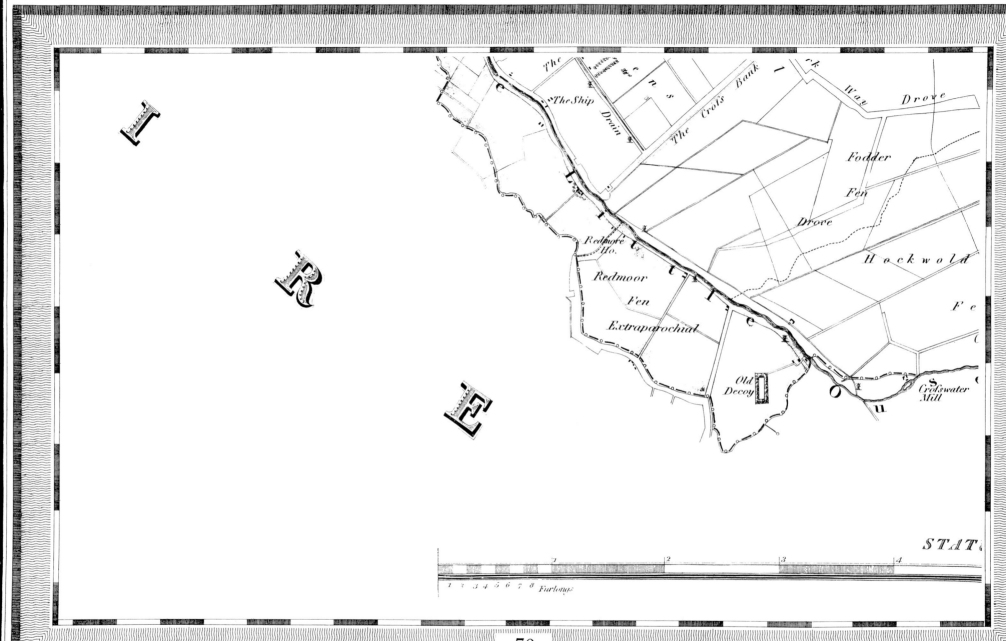

I R E

The Ship

The Crofs Bank

Way Drove

Fodder Fen Drove

Redmore Ho.

Redmoor Fen

Extraparochial

Hockwold

Old Decoy

Crofswater Mill

STAT

1   2   3   4

1 2 3 4 5 6 7 8 *Furlongs*

H U N D R E

S

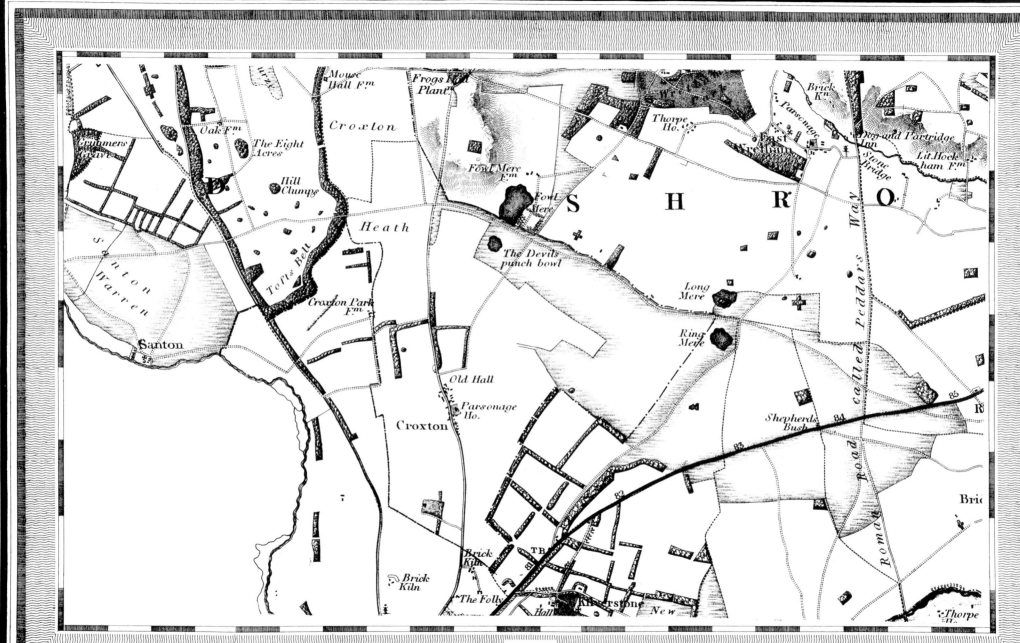

Grimmers Grave

Oak Fm

The Eight Acres

Mouse Hall Fm

Frogs Hill Plant

Croxton

Hill Clumps

Fowl Mere Fm

Heath

Tofts Belt

Fowl Mere

B

Santon Warren

Croxton Park Fm

The Devils punch bowl

Long Mere

Ring Mere

Santon

Old Hall

Parsonage Ho.

Croxton

Brick Kiln

Brick Kiln

The Folly

Hall

T.B

Thetford New

West

Thorpe Ho.

East Wretham

Parsonage

Brick Kn.

Dog and Partridge Inn

Stone Bridge

Lit Hockham Fm

S H R O

Shepherds Bush

Road called Peddars Way

Roman

85

84

83

82

Brid

Thorpe

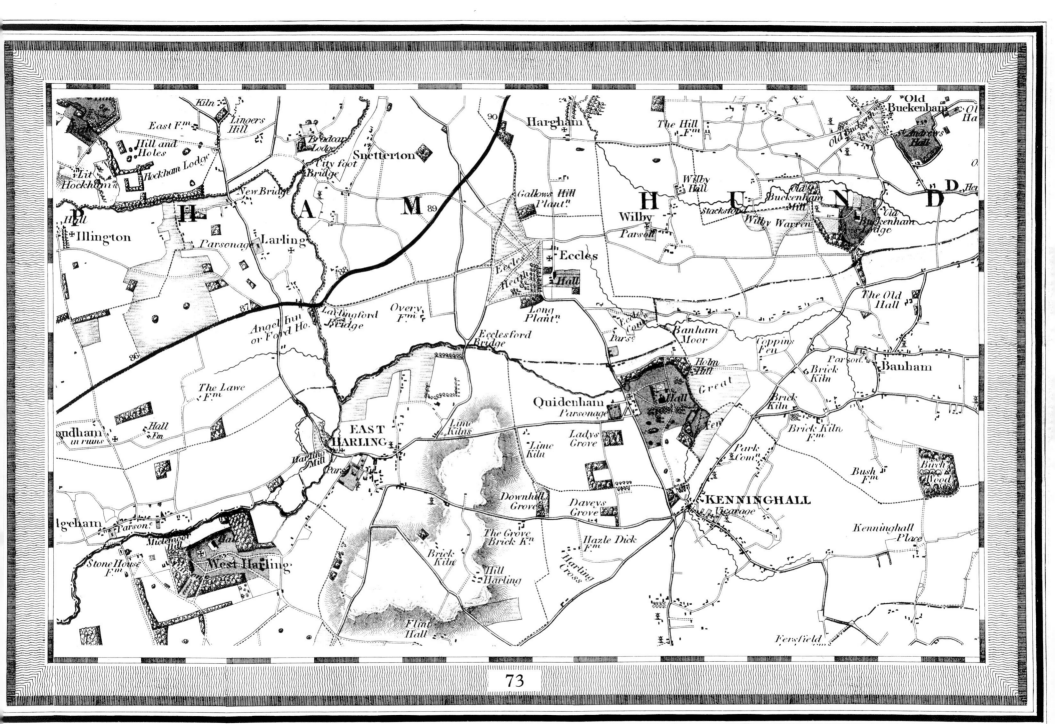

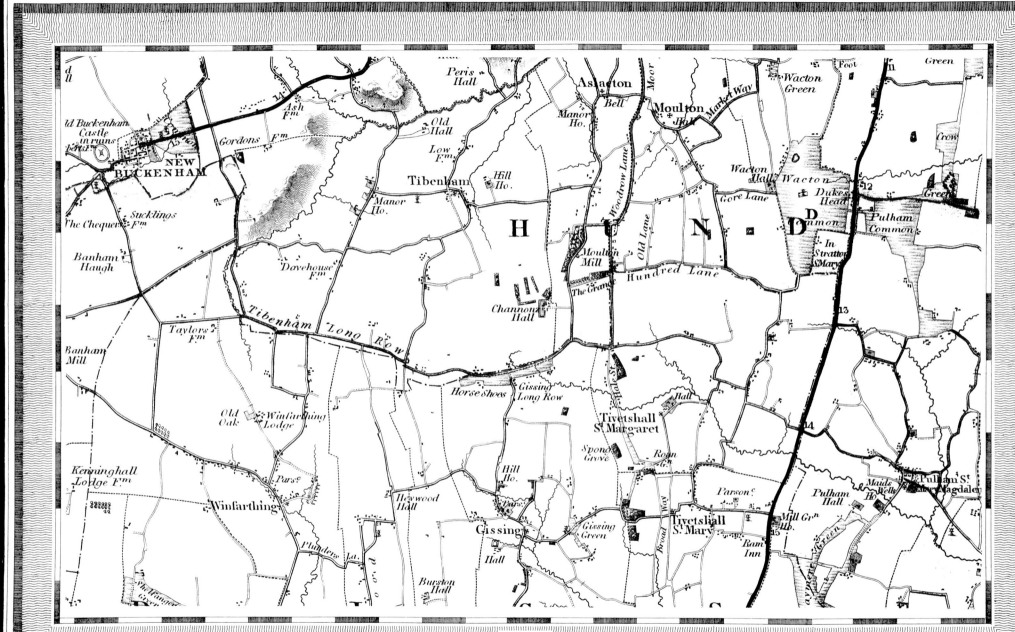

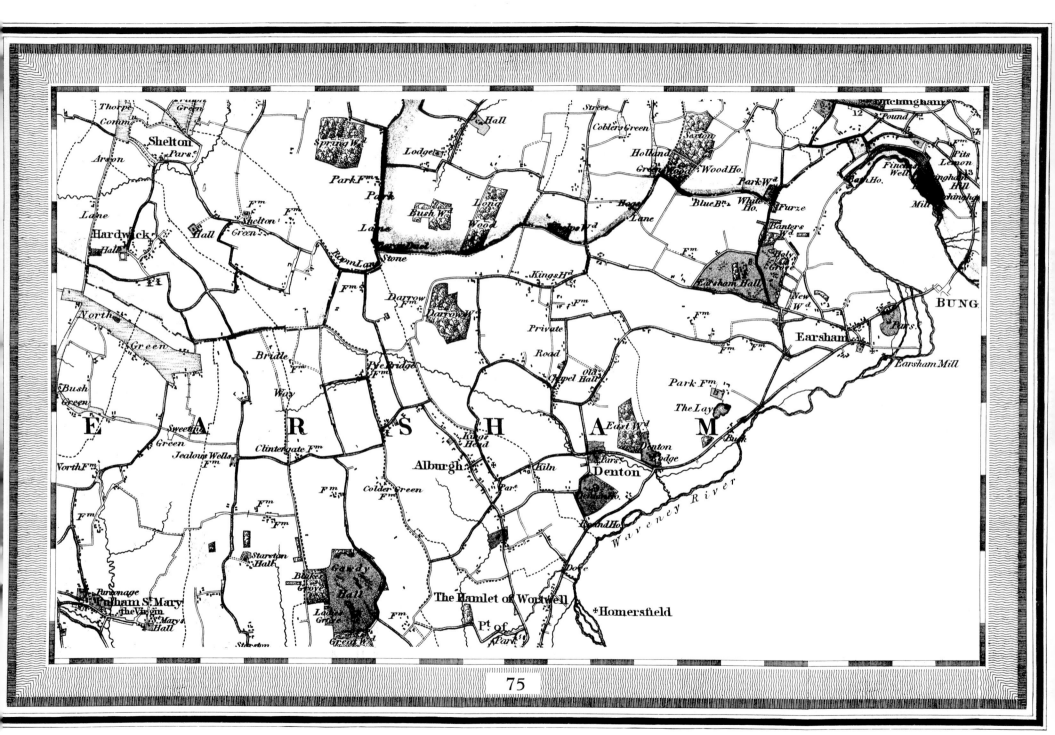

Thorpe Comm.
Green
Shelton
Pars.
Arson
Shelton
Lane
Green
Hardwick
Hall
Hall
Fm
Fm

Spring Wd
Park Fm
Park
Lane
Bush Wd
Long Wood
Room Lane
Stone

Hall
Lodge

Street
Coblers Green
Saxton
Holland
Green
Wood Ho.
Park Wd
Blue Brs.
White Ho.
Furze
Banters Wd
Earsham Hall
Holy Grn.
New Wd

Pound
Finches Well
Mill
Pits Lemon
Hill
BUNGAY

North
Green
Bush
Green
E   A   R   S   H   A   M

Darrow
Darrow Wd
Kings Hd
Private
Road
Chapel Hall
Old Hall
Fm
Fm
East Wd
Park Fm
The Lay
Earsham
Earsham Mill

Bridle
Way
Pye Bridge
Sweethen
Green
Jealous Wells
Clintergate Fm
Fm

Alburgh
Kings
Head
Kiln
Pars.
Denton
Denton
Lodge
Buck

North Fm
Fm
Fm
Fm
Fm
Colder Green
Fm
Par.
Ho.
Pond Ho.

Waveney River

Starston
Hall
Bucks
Grove
Gawdy
Hall
Pulham St Mary
the Virgin
Parsonage
St Mary's Hall
Lady
Grove
Starston
Great Wd
The Hamlet of Wortwell
Dove
Homersfield
Pt of
Park

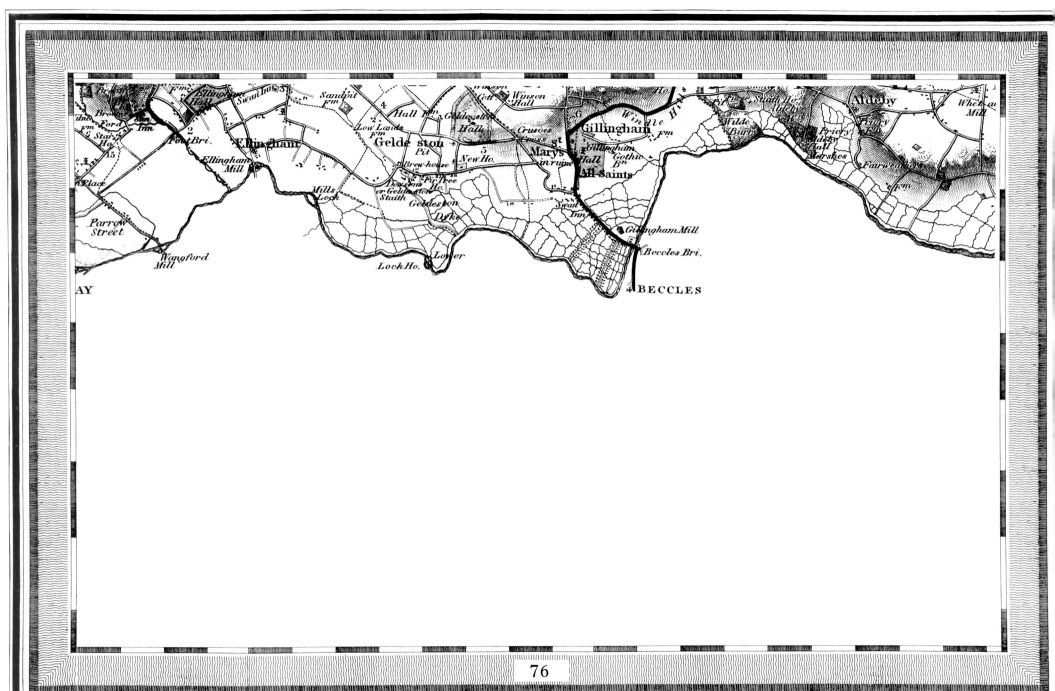

AY

Bro...
Bro...
...ihe
Ford
Inn
Star
Ho.
15
...Place

Parrow
Street

Wangford
Mill

Ellingham
Hall
2
Foot Bri.
Ellingham
Ellingham
Mill

Swan Ino. 3
Sandpit
Fm.

Low Lands
Fm.
Pit
Brew-house
Dosens
or Geldeston
Staith

Mills
Lock

Geldeston
Dyke

Lock Ho.

Lower

Hall Fm.
Geldeston
Hall
Gelde ston
4

Fir-Tree
Ho.

5
New Ho.

Winson
Cott.
Winson
Hall

Crusoes

Marys
in ruins

Swan
Inn

6
Gillingham
Fm.

Gillingham
Gothic
Br.

Gillingham
Hall
All saints

1 H

Windle Hl.

Gillingham Mill

Beccles Bri.

BECCLES

Ho.

Fm.
South Ho.
Wilde
Bury

Priory
Ho.
Aldeby
Hall
Marshes

Aldeby
Priory
Ho.

Fairweather

Wheat
Mill

Fm.

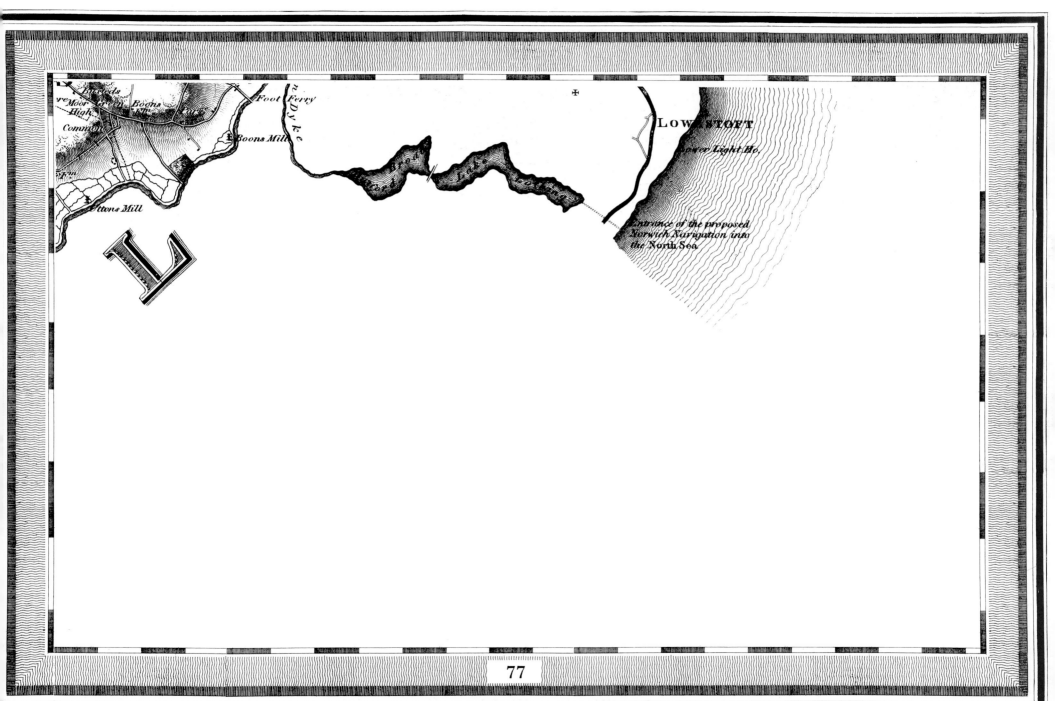

Buck'ds

Moor High

Common

Boons Mill

Foot Ferry

n Dyke

ttons Mill

LOWESTOFT

wer Light Ho.

ntrance of the proposed
Norwich Navigation into
the North Sea

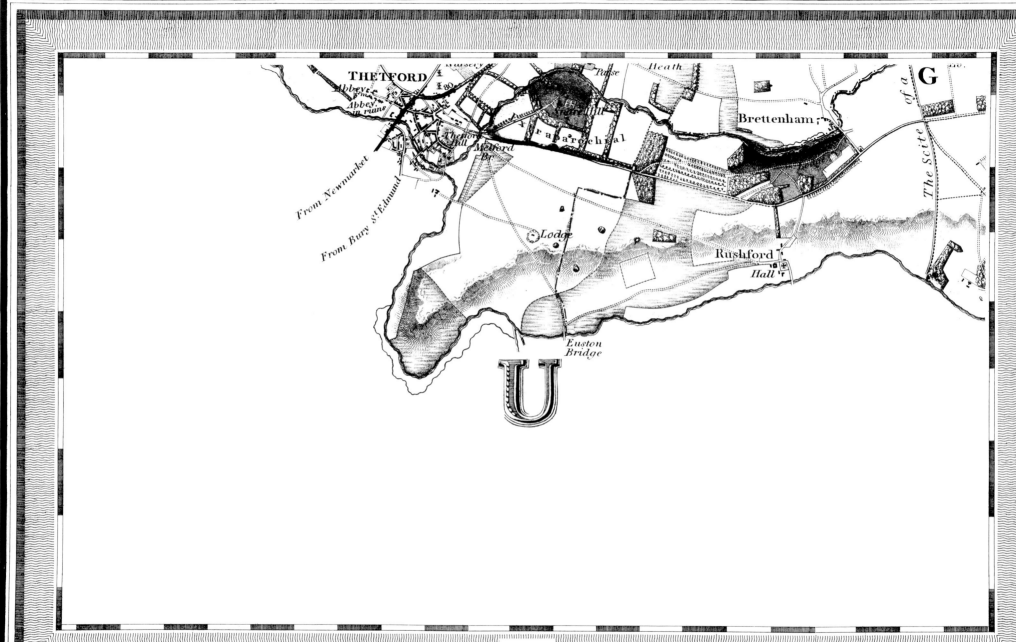

THETFORD

Abbey
Abbey in ruins

Nursery

Pause
Heath

Brettenham

From Newmarket

Thetford Hill Melford Br

From Bury St Edmund

a paroch al

Lodge

Rushford

Hall

Euston
Bridge

The Scite of a

G

U

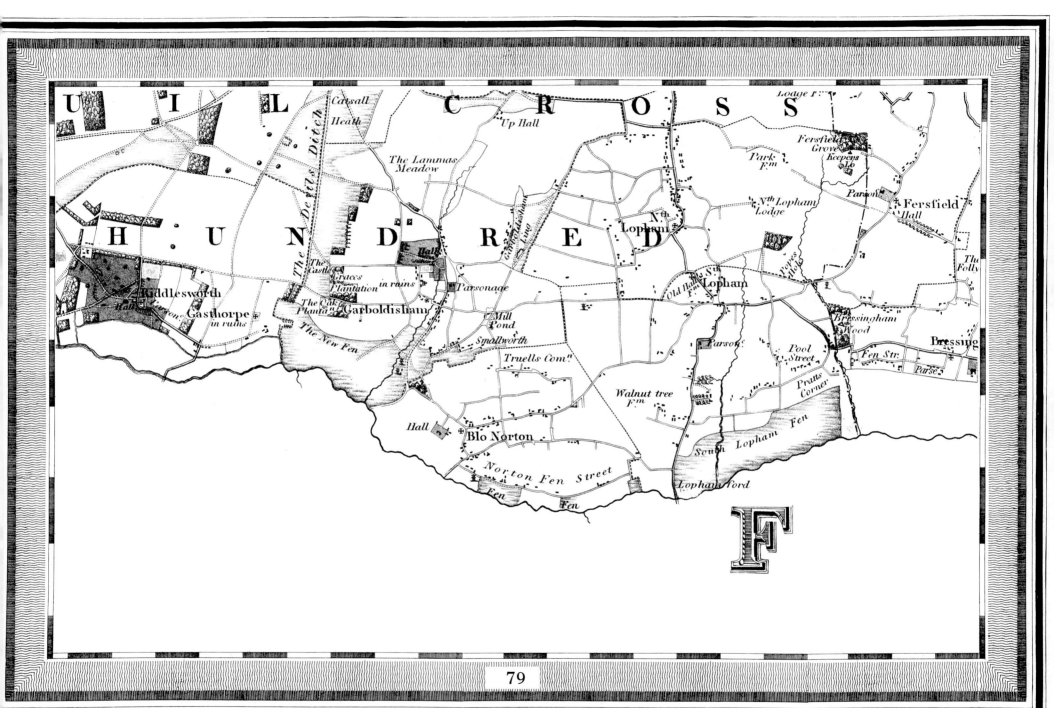

GUILCROSS HUNDRED

Catsall Heath
Up Hall
The Lammas Meadow
Devil's Ditch
The Castle
Graces Plantation in ruins
Hall
Parsonage
The Oak Plant
Riddlesworth
Hall
Barrow
Gasthorpe *in ruins*
Garboldisham
The New Fen
Mill Pond
Smallworth
Truells Com
Hall
Blo Norton
Norton Fen Street
Fen
Fen
Walnut tree Fm
Gunghersham Lug
Lodge F
Fersfield Grove
Keepers Lo
Park Fm
Nth Lopham Lodge
Nth Lopham
Parson
Fersfield Hall
The Folly
Old Hall Fm
Hall Str
Lopham
Popes Moke
Parson
Pool Street
Pratts Corner
South Lopham Fen
Lopham ford
Bressingham Wood
Fen Str
Bressing
Parso

F

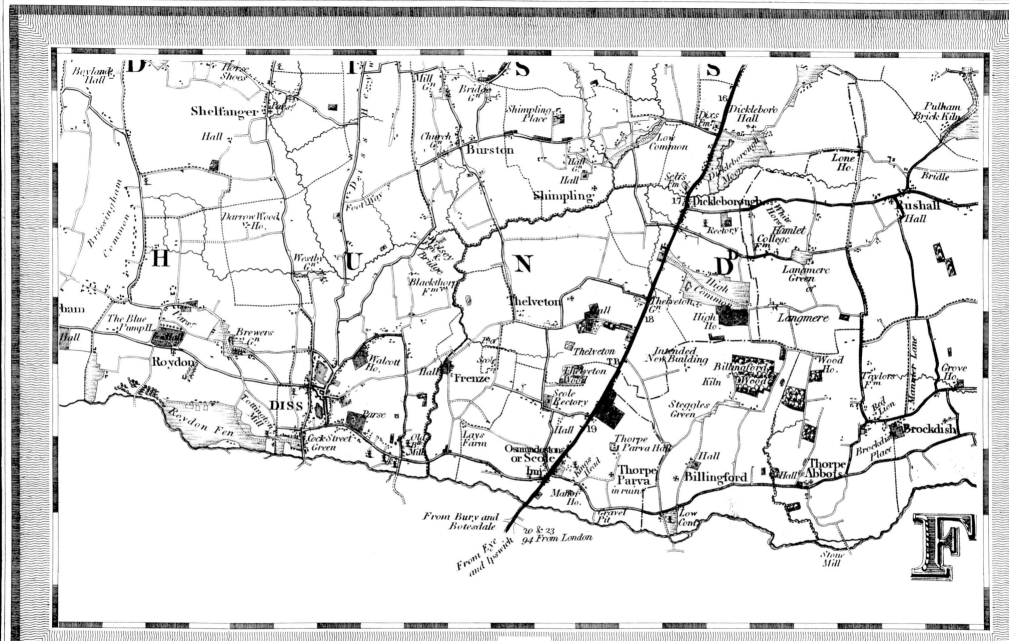

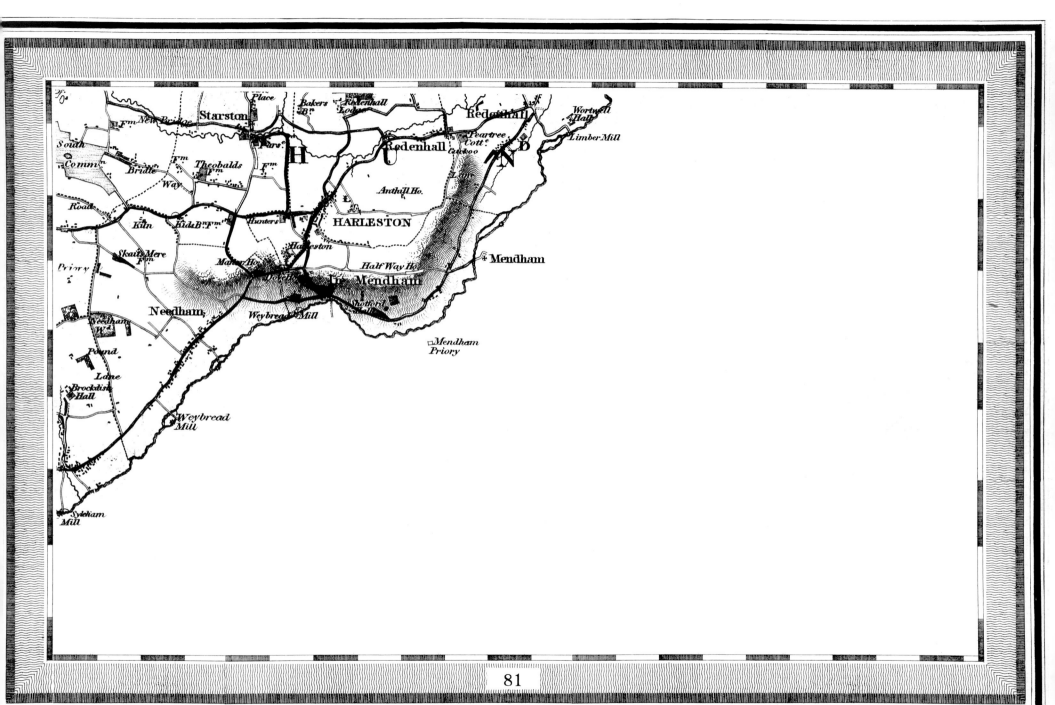

A List of Bryant's County Maps

Hertfordshire 1822
Surrey 1823
Oxfordshire 1824
Buckinghamshire 1825
Suffolk 1826 (March)
Bedfordshire 1826 (September)
Norfolk 1826 (December)
Northamptonshire 1827
Lincolnshire 1828
East Riding of Yorkshire 1829
Cheshire 1831
Herefordshire 1835

Copies of all these maps are held in the Royal Geographical Society Map Room.
Thanks are due to the staff of the Map Room for producing all these maps for examination.